GREAT COMMISSION OBEDIENCE

The Road to Resurgence

JERRY RANKIN

PUBLISHING GROUP
Nashville, Tennessee

ISBN: 978-0-8054-4879-5

Published by B&H Publishing Group,
Nashville, Tennessee

Dewey Decimal Classification: 266.023
Subject Heading: FOREIGN MISSIONS

1 2 3 4 5 6 7 8 9 10 • 15 14 13 12 11

CONTENTS

FOREWORD

I will never forget the message that Baker James Cauthen, then president of the Foreign Mission Board, preached when my wife and I were appointed as missionaries. God spoke to us and reaffirmed our calling that night through Dr. Cauthen's words of challenge. He also used that message to touch the hearts of our family and friends. We have often looked back on that night as one of the markers God has given us of His call on our lives. After we completed our service on the mission field, the call continued as I worked with missionary candidates and appointees for more than twenty-five years.

Does God still use the commissioning messages that are preached during missionary appointment services? The answer is an unequivocal "yes!" For the past seventeen years, I have witnessed how He has used Jerry Rankin, former president of the International Mission Board, to speak to the hearts of appointees and to everyone attending those services. Dr. Rankin preaches with a passion that comes from God's Word, his own call to missions, and his many years of service on the mission field. His messages also come out of his experience leading the IMB during its time of greatest growth—a time when more people have been saved and baptized, more churches planted, and more missionaries sent from Southern Baptist churches than ever before.

I am honored to introduce Dr. Rankin's second volume of commissioning messages, *Great Commission Obedience*. I commend it to you as inspiring devotional reading and as a great resource for scriptural messages on missions and mission illustrations. These are messages that God has used to motivate thousands of listeners. I am confident He will use them to inspire you as you read them.

Lloyd Atkinson, former Vice-President
Office of Missionary Personnel
International Mission Board, SBC

PREFACE

If there is any passage of Scripture familiar to most evangelical Christians—next to John 3:16—it would be the Great Commission in Matthew 28:19–20. This record of Jesus' concluding challenge to His disciples before He ascended to the Father was a mandate to go and make disciples of all nations. Although the terminology of "great commission" is not found in the biblical passage itself, it has come to be identified with this command of our Lord as a compelling task that is pre-eminent in fulfilling the mission of God.

Linked with parallel references to be witnesses "to the ends of the earth" (Acts 1:8), "go into all the world and preach the gospel to the whole creation" (Mark 16:15) and others, the Great Commission is variously interpreted as a command to witness and win the lost to saving faith in Jesus Christ. One would think that any committed Christian would be conscientious about being obedient to what our Lord has commanded us to do, but we readily dismiss our negligence to disciple the nations by skillful rationalization and hermeneutical manipulation.

Many reason that the Great Commission is whatever we happen to do in witness and ministry. Others justify failure to go to the nations by assuming we only have a responsibility to witness to the lost where we live. Ignoring the fact that Jesus was outlining the progressive advance of the gospel in the first century, it has been common to interpret the Acts 1:8 passage to give priority to local missions. It is assumed there is no compelling obligation to reach the ends of the earth until we have completed the task within the concentric circles closer to home.

Rather than a compelling priority for His disciples and successive generations of believers, many treat the Great Commission as if it were an afterthought. They picture Jesus on a mountaintop in Galilee enjoying a final time of earthly fellowship with His followers. Jesus says rather passively, "Oh, by the way, it just occurred to me—why don't you go and make disciples of other nations." To the contrary, the mission to disciple the nations was born in the heart of God before the foundation of the world and was passionately reflected in the life and message of Jesus throughout His earthly ministry.

Jesus did not introduce the concept of the Great Commission upon completion of His time upon earth but ratified this as the eternal will and purpose of the Father. It was the reason God had called Abraham to leave his home and family, "and all the peoples on earth will be blessed through you" (Gen. 12:3). The Great Commission was the purpose for which God raised up a chosen people, Israel, to "proclaim His salvation from day to day; declare His glory among the nations, His wonderful works among all peoples" (1 Chron. 16:23–24).

Jesus came declaring He had come "to seek and save the lost" (Luke 19:10) and then relegated that task to His disciples: "As the Father has sent Me, I also send you" (Jn 20:21). Even His death and resurrection was not just to save those of us who believe, but to provide a message of salvation to be proclaimed to the whole world. He defied any possibility of an ego-centric perspective of our salvation in explaining to His disciples the rationale of why He died and rose again. "This is what is written: the Messiah would suffer and rise from the dead the third day, and repentance for forgiveness of sin would be proclaimed in His name to all the nations" (Luke 24:46–47).

So that final mandate in Matthew 28:19–20 was not just the introduction of a new task; it was a reminder and final commissioning of a task that had already been clearly defined and articulated throughout the biblical narrative. Whether one interprets it from a narrow local perspective of witness and ministry or from the broader global perspective of reaching the nations, the Great Commission is not optional. It is not a specialized task for an elite force of missionaries but marching orders to the church and people of God.

There has been a renewed consciousness of the need to give greater priority to fulfilling this mandate of our Lord and become more aligned with the mission of God to the nations. While we are expected to be faithful in our witness and discipling those where we live, we cannot ignore the fact that the objective of the Great Commission is the nations—the "*panta ta ethne*" or peoples of the world. A Great Commission resurgence implies a renewed emphasis on something that was once surging but has now waned. Whether or not this mission of discipling the nations was ever truly effective in the contemporary church, there is no question regarding the need for a renewed emphasis and endeavor in the task.

Many have been resistant to making changes in the status quo of church and denominational programs in order to make more resources available to missions. While acknowledging the need to do more to reach a lost world, stimulate evangelistic activity and enhance church growth, the task is seen as a spiritual one that is contingent on God choosing to bless and empower our activity. This results in a passive deflection of personal responsibility while waiting for God to ignite a fire of passion in the hearts and lives of His people.

This attitude seems to ignore the fact that God's blessing follows obedience. First John 3:22 reminds us that we "receive whatever we ask from Him because we keep His command and do what is pleasing in His sight." Why would we wait expectantly for God to bless disobedience and neglect? The possibility that He would bless us and answer our prayers for spiritual renewal and reaching the lost is contingent on our obedience to what He has clearly told us to do.

Jesus tells an interesting parable in Matthew 21:28–31 of two sons. "But what do you think? A man had two sons, and he came to the first and said, 'Son, go work today in the vineyard.' And he answered and said, 'I will, sir'; and he did not go. And he came to the second and said the same thing. But he answered and said, "I will not'; yet he afterward regretted it and went. Which of the two did the will of his father?"

Jesus did not elaborate on this story or provide an explanation or application. Instead he posed the question to His listeners by asking them "What do you think?" and then left the conclusion lingering for them to interpret which son was obedient—the one who actually did the work or the one whose commitment to obedience was mere rhetoric.

It is a parallel of our response to what God has told us to do as His children. We have been told to go and work in the fields that are white unto harvest. We are to disciple the nations and claim the kingdoms of the world as the kingdom of our Lord. In all of the debate about a Great Commission Resurgence, we may define it in different ways to apply to the lost where we live, to intensify evangelistic activity or send more missionaries to reach the nations, but we have to acknowledge this is what our Father has told us to do.

Are we truly obedient in the task or is our obedience not much more than rhetoric? Southern Baptists like to think of themselves as a Great Commission people who give priority to missions. We talk about all the effective programs in the local church and among convention entities as "missions" and doing what our Lord has told us to do. But baptisms are in decline, churches plateaued and dying, little progress is being made in penetrating the lostness of America and so many peoples around the world have yet to be engaged with a Christian witness. Are we not like the first son? We proclaim allegiance to the Great Commission, but we are not really engaged in the work.

Obedience is more than giving lip-service to the task. We can confess an understanding of the Great Commission and commitment to it, but never get around to actually doing it. Men and women in military service are trained to be obedient to their orders without question. It would be unthinkable, and bring immediate consequences of court martial, if they ignored or acted contrary to what they had been commanded to do. It is tragic that so many consider optional being obedient to the orders of our commander-in-chief, Jesus Christ, who has told us to go into all the world and make disciples of all nations.

Obedience doesn't happen by default or from a passive regard of what we should be doing. It doesn't happen by just acknowledging the task. There has to be an intentionality and commitment to working in the field. Pastors appeal to their congregation and people in attendance regularly to nail down a spiritual marker of commitment by making a public decision. Mere contemplation or discussion of the need doesn't make an impact on lostness. There has to be a commitment to action.

Likewise, obedience doesn't come without a cost. The obedient son had to give up his own plans. We don't know why he initially refused to go and work in the vineyard, but it was probably because he was already busy with other things or pre-occupied with his own plans and agenda for the day. We cannot just keep on doing all that we are doing and think we can be obedient in reaching a lost world. If our priorities are to change, it means we will have to give up something else and sacrifice what we might prefer to be doing personally. We will not reach a lost world by continuing business and usual. We have got to be willing to give up something if changes are to be made in order to be obedient to our Great Commission task.

It remains to be seen whether Southern Baptists will see a refocus of resources, give priority to missions and evangelism and see a resurgence in reaching the nations. But many individuals, families and churches are reflecting the model of the obedient son. A new generation of missionaries are turning their backs on personal comforts and security to go to the ends of the earth. They are leaving promising careers and successful ministries to go to the nations. They are engaging unreached people groups with an evangelistic witness for the first time and seeing an accelerating harvest throughout the world.

It has been my privilege as president of the International Mission Board for seventeen years to see more than ten thousand missionary personnel commissioned to overseas ministry. Six times a year a group of career missionaries are appointed to a lifetime of service on foreign fields. They face the challenge of language learning and cultural adjustments isolated from friends and family. They embrace austere life-styles, face hostility and harassment and risk persecution and danger for the sake of the gospel. But they go with a personal conviction of God's call and in obedience to the Great Commission.

The messages in this book are a selection of those used in more than a hundred services to appoint, commission and challenge these new missionaries. Although the text and outlines are unique, readers will note a parallel in content and even repetition in some of the illustrations used since each message was delivered in different locations, among different audiences and groups of missionary candidates. Regardless the occasion and where missionaries may be deployed, factors involved in obedience to the Great Commission remain constant.

Obedience means coming to the point of saying, "not my will but Thine be done." It is essential that one be willing to lay personal desires and plans on the altar, crucify any aspirations for reputation and success, and die to self-interest in order to follow God's will.

One must walk by faith and maintain an uncommon devotion to God. Obedience requires total dependence on His power and the discipline to maintain an intimate relationship with the source of power that flows from His Spirit.

Obedience also invariably entails suffering. One would think a commitment to serve God and sacrifice personal desires and comforts would be recompensed by a divine hedge of protection that would keep one from illness and tragedy. To the contrary, suffering goes with the task and is a consequence of venturing into Satan's territory to claim the kingdoms of the world as the kingdom of our Lord. Persevering in suffering and sacrifice is often the most effective witness of the reality of a living Savior to a lost world.

These and other themes emerge in each message and reinforce the realities of God's Word and teachings of the One who calls His people to obedience. These are challenges, not only to missionaries being commissioned to overseas service, but to any Christian who is conscientious about following our Lord in obedience. If we are to take the road to resurgence in winning the lost and reaching a lost world these messages must be a reflection of the obedience of every Christian and church member.

I would be gratified for pastors to see these messages as a resource to challenge their own people to Great Commission obedience. I'm convinced many pastors fail to preach consistently on missions because they do not recognize the missionary message inherent in many passages of Scripture. I pray the messages selected for this volume will find a relevancy as local churches send out mission teams, dedicate their own missionaries, ordain deacons and pastors and install church leadership for the qualifications for obedient service are the same.

I appreciate the staff of B&H Publishing Group; they have been an encouragement and partner in producing this volume of messages. This is a sequel to an earlier publication by B&H in 2006,

The Challenge to Great Commission Obedience. Thoroughly biblical and packed with practical mission stories and illustrations, these messages reflect what it means to be obedient to the Great Commission. It is my joy to share them with a wider audience in hopes it might be a resource, along with others, guiding us on the road to resurgence.

Don't Nullify God's Grace 10/9

Ephesians 3:7–8

As we respond to the challenge of obedience to the Great Commission, it is natural to focus on the future and the place to which God would use us in discipling the nations. While we do not go out of obligation in response to a command, Jesus clearly expected His followers to be engaged in taking the gospel to the peoples of the world. No one is exempt from the task of bringing into the kingdom people from every tribe, language, and nation and discipling them to become followers of Christ. For some the task involves sending, praying, and giving; but the Great Commission will not be fulfilled without those willing to go to the ends of the earth.

A focus on Great Commission obedience is usually from a future perspective. Where am I to go? What does God want me to do? Where does He want me to serve? Anticipating being used of God in a significant way means a willingness to follow wherever He leads, but first we need to reflect on what has brought you to this point of obedience and review from whence you have come.

WE ARE QUALIFIED BY BEING A RECIPIENT OF GOD'S GRACE

God has brought you to this point, not because of your own abilities or qualifications, though you have fulfilled certain standards of education, experience, and personal competency. However, the potential of being used to meet the Great Commission challenge is not because of your education, experience, and personality; it is because of the grace of God. Certainly others have invested in your life in providing discipline, training, influence, and in exposing you to the needs of a lost world. However, in spite of all those factors, you are primarily qualified because of the grace of God.

In Ephesians 3:7–8, Paul says, "I was made a servant of this [gospel] by the gift of God's grace that was given to me by the working of His power. This grace was given to me—the least of all the saints!—to proclaim to the Gentiles the incalculable riches of the Messiah."

1. Recognize, first of all, that you are qualified to fulfill the Great Commission because of the grace of God which saved you. At some point He brought you under the conviction of sin and enabled you to understand His saving grace in Jesus Christ. As unworthy as you were, God chose to save you, not because of your own righteousness, but because of His grace.

2. Second, His grace called you according to the working of His power. There came a time when your will became submissive to what God was leading you to do, but you have not come to this point as a result of your own decision as if you simply chose to become a missionary. You were chosen by God's grace, and He would not let you do otherwise.

3. Third, God's grace determined His purpose for your life. You may be going to places you would never have dreamed of and perhaps have never heard of. You are going to fill a particular assignment that fits with your gifts and experience because that is who God made you to be. He shaped your life for this purpose through His grace.

The location and assignment for your place in fulfilling the Great Commission is unique and distinct from others, but the purpose for which He has called you is the same. As Paul described that purpose, it is to preach the unsearchable riches of Christ. Regardless of your assignment or job description, that is the purpose for which His grace has called you.

4. And finally, I want to remind you, that His grace will empower you for the task. It is not your own ability or ingenuity; not your competency, training, and skills. If you are to be used effectively in making Christ known, you must always be cognizant that it is due to His grace using your life as a channel of witness and power.

The apostle Paul was used mightily of God because he was constantly aware that he was totally dependent on God's grace. Note another word of testimony in 1 Corinthians 15:10, "But by God's grace I am what I am, and His grace toward me was not ineffective. However, I worked more than any of them, yet not I, but God's grace that was with me."

Paul's testimony in Galatians 2:19–20 is one of the most graphic and powerful expressions of the Christian experience. He proclaims, "I have been crucified with Christ; and I no longer live, but Christ lives in me. The life I now live in the flesh, I live by faith in the Son of God, who loved me and gave Himself for me." On the basis of this he follows by saying, "I do not set aside the grace of God."

THE DANGER OF GOD'S GRACE BEING NULLIFIED

Grace is the undeserved favor of God. He has saved us and called us by His grace, through no merit of our own whatsoever. He promises to lead us and empower us by His grace; in fact, the life of Christ Himself is poured into ours to do it all—live our life for us. But note that it is highly possible that that grace may be in vain. It is not unlikely that you will get to the place where God has called you to impact a lost world and nullify the rich, abundant, free-flowing, powerful grace of God which is available to empower and use you.

That is not the grace of God which saved you—praise God that can't be nullified or canceled—but the grace of God which has chosen you and called you. The grace needed to make Christ known, and the grace that represents the spiritual power to transcend cultures and break through barriers of sin and pride can be forfeited. The power which Jesus promised with the indwelling presence of the Holy Spirit equips you to be His witnesses. It is possible for all of that grace to be of no effect.

1. Failure to be focused and single-minded. First, you may render God's grace of no effect if you fail to be single-minded and totally devoted to the task to which God has called you. Satan will provide many diversions that will demand your time and attention. Many of them are good and worthwhile activities, but they will divert you from your primary purpose for being there of making Christ known. You will immediately get caught up in cultural adjustments and language learning; you will spend time and energy providing for the comforts and the needs of your family. You will be involved in committee meetings, fulfilling recreational needs, responding to the urgent demands around you; and one day you will realize there is no evidence of God's grace bringing lost souls to Jesus Christ.

2. Failure to persevere and be obedient. Second, you can nullify the grace of God by your failure to be obedient and persevere through times of difficulty and crisis. Be assured those times will come; they go with the territory. Life on the mission field will not be easy. There will be occasions when you wonder why you are there and question why you have subjected your family and children to such hardship. Perhaps you will not readily find acceptance and response; rejection and persecution should always be seen as a possibility.

Some time ago I counseled with a missionary family who had experienced a very frustrating first term and felt they could be used more effectively somewhere else. I agreed and began to discuss the options for an alternate assignment. They interrupted me and said, "But we want you to know that we are willing to return here." I was surprised, having assumed they were unwilling to face the same frustration and difficulties of another term, but they explained, "When we arrived and realized what we were up against, we had to reconcile ourselves to the fact that God had not called us to happiness or personal fulfillment but to obedience. And if this is where He wants us, we want to be obedient."

3. Failure to live a cleansed, pure life. Third, you can nullify the grace of God and render it of no effect by failure to live a cleansed, pure life. We don't like to talk about this, but there have been missionaries whose service has been in vain because they did not maintain a holy walk before the Lord. As missionary families pack their crate for overseas shipment, it seems that VCRs have become standard equipment. We justify that by our need for relaxation and diversion, for staying in touch with our American roots. But let me warn you that you don't subject your mind to the filth and garbage of contemporary society and entertainment without compromising the flow of God's grace. We are told that our bodies are the temple of the living God, and we are to separate ourselves, to cleanse ourselves from all defilement of flesh and spirit, perfecting holiness in the fear of God. God expects you to walk in purity, not just physically abstaining from immoral indulgence and influence, but in spirit and attitude and in relationships lest His grace be in vain.

4. Failure to respond appropriately to adversity. Fourth, you can nullify the grace of God which He promised to make available by failing to respond appropriately to adversity. Every day we receive news of those among our global missionary family who have been afflicted with severe illness, injured in an accident, suffered the loss of a parent or loved one far away. There are those who live without electricity or in isolation from the supportive fellowship of Christian colleagues. You are joining this group, and you, too, will experience adversity. You can feel sorry for yourself, resent your circumstances, get angry with God, criticize the Foreign Mission Board, and nullify the grace of God that is available to see you through. Or you can respond in faith, learn what God is teaching you, rely upon His strength, and find His grace to be sufficient.

5. Failure to trust God and walk by faith. Finally, you can nullify the grace of God by failing to trust Him and, instead, following your own wisdom and understanding. Unfortunately, we don't have very accurate insights into the future due to our limited human vision. And that is how it should be. Proverbs 3:5–6 tells us, "Trust in the LORD with all your heart, and do not rely on your own understanding; think about Him in all your ways, and He will guide you on the right paths."

We must trust God, acknowledge His lordship, allow Him to lead in all our ways with assurance He will direct our paths and provide all the grace needed for the task to which He called us. We experience that grace for guidance only when we follow by faith.

Jonah 2:8 makes the observation, "Those who cling to worthless idols forfeit the grace that could be theirs" (NIV). We recognize the foolishness of forfeiting the precious grace of God for salvation by clinging to worthless idols. But let me urge you not to forfeit the abundant grace of God, which is sufficient for your every need and will empower you in witness and ministry. It would be equally foolish to forfeit God's grace by clinging to your own understanding and failing to trust God, by failing to respond in faith in times of adversity, by failing to live a cleansed, pure life, by failing to be obedient and single-minded in your commitment to God's will and calling.

You have been saved and called by God's grace. Don't nullify the grace He provides to carry out the Great Commission as you go in obedience to His call.

That They Would See Jesus

Luke 24:31

God has called every church and every believer to be obedient to the Great Commission. No one is exempt from the responsibility our Lord has given to His followers to make disciples of all nations. Truly a heart for the world should be reflected in our cooperative support in making Christ known to every people, tribe, tongue, and nation. The task is far from complete, and while God calls all of us to pray and to give, we should bring to Him a surrendered heart and readiness to go that a lost world would know God's love and come to faith in our Lord Jesus Christ. God continues to call out those to plant their lives overseas among people who are lost in obedience to the Great Commission.

We must uphold the missionaries going in response to God's call with prayer and give to support their ministry and witness overseas. In God's divine providence they have a personal sense of call to the places to which they are being appointed. Some are going to highly responsive countries in Africa and Latin America such as Kenya, Tanzania, Malawi, Uganda, Venezuela, and Brazil. Others are going to impact the burgeoning population of Taiwan, Hong Kong, Indonesia, and Thailand, or to pioneer outreach among relatively untouched people groups in Central Asia, North Africa, and the Middle East. A significant number are responding to the urgent call to seize the opportunity to impact Europe with the gospel in this era of transition.

Although they are filling a variety of assignments, all strategic to the total missions task, Luke 24:31 clearly defines the purpose for which these are being appointed tonight. This is the account of the resurrection appearance of Jesus to the two men on the road to Emmaus. Jesus had conversed with them throughout the journey about the events of the preceding days and how the Scriptures had explained the necessity of His death and resurrection. They did not know it was Jesus until they entered into a home and were dining. Jesus blessed the food, and the Scripture says, "Then their eyes were opened, and they recognized Him" (Luke 24:31).

That is why you are being commissioned tonight—that the eyes of a lost world might be opened, and they would recognize Jesus. You may be going to serve as teachers, as a doctor, hospital administrator, or in development work. Many of you will be filling the broad responsibilities of a church and home assignment. But the reason you are going to places such as Ghana, Mali, Romania, Belarus, and Serbia is so that the eyes of a lost world will be opened, and they will see Jesus.

Some of you are going to the Buddhist countries of Asia where people believe that the goal and destiny of their soul will be realized as a result of good works. The spires of Buddhist pagodas, ornate temples, and spirit houses attest to the prolific devotion to a misguided philosophy, which fails to comprehend that the soul that sins shall die (Rom. 3:23). These are a beautiful, hospitable and gracious people, who believe their eternal destiny is determined by their own good works. But the futility of their religious traditions are evident when one attends a funeral and observes the saffron-robed priests encircling the casket, chanting, "Dead, never to arise; asleep never to awaken; gone never to return." They see Jesus as a great teacher and philosopher, but God has called you to open their eyes that they might recognize Jesus as none other than the unique, glorified Son of God, the Savior of the world.

Others will be witnessing among the Hindu masses of South Asia who know Jesus as only one among their millions of deities. You will be overwhelmed by the multitudes and the density of population where more than a billion people live in a land area approximately one-third the size of the United States. As you respond with compassion in ministry and witness to the needs, you genuinely want to relieve the suffering of this mass of humanity. But the compelling reason you go is so that their eyes would be opened to recognize Jesus as "the way, the truth, and the life," declaring that "no man cometh unto the Father, but by me" (John 14:6 KJV).

There are those in these Hindu areas who will readily respond to your witness and accept Jesus but add Him to their pantheon of gods. They are delighted to find a potential Savior to relieve them of the endless cycle of reincarnations imposed as retribution for deeds in a former life. But their eyes, blinded to the truth, need to be opened to see Jesus as the unique, sinless Son of God who alone died for the sins of the world.

You are going to places in the Middle East and North Africa where 950 million Muslims have been resistant to the Christian message; they recognize Jesus as a prophet but nothing more. The cry from minarets reverberates throughout the countryside, calling the people to prayer to affirm their belief there is but one God, Allah, and Mohammed is his prophet. You will never get used to that sound offending your ears and piercing your heart as a repetitive reminder of your task to open their eyes that they might recognize Jesus and that in His name alone are salvation and eternal life.

They have been convinced that the Bible has been corrupted and that an imposter, someone other than Jesus, died on the cross. They do not accept the Trinitarian nature of God but see this Christian teaching as a blasphemous offense to their monotheistic faith. The truth has been obscured; their fatalistic devotion to an impersonal god has blinded their eyes to the fact that God is love and became a man in order to die for their sins.

Almost two thousand years ago, Jesus told us to "go into all the world and preach the gospel to the whole creation" (Mark 16:15). Yet researchers have been able to identify 1.2 billion people among the nations and ethnic groups that have yet to hear the name of Jesus. They are isolated culturally and geographically among people groups where there are no churches, no Christian to be a witness within their society, no Bibles in their language; they have not yet been engaged with a missionary witness. The Bible describes them as in darkness, without hope and alienated from God.

The men on the road to Emmaus had been among the crowd of believers who followed Jesus, but in their grief in seeing Him die, they were so dismayed and disillusioned they were unable to recognize Him. However, multitudes today do not recognize Him because no one has ever told them who Jesus is. Like these disciples who, in God's divine timing, had their eyes opened to recognize Jesus, it is God's desire that all the world would see Jesus. We are told He is "not wanting any to perish, but all to come to repentance" (2 Pet. 3:9). You are being sent to the unevangelized, untouched peoples that they might be turned from darkness to light and from the power of Satan unto God.

This was Paul's way of describing the challenge to Great Commission obedience. As he testified before King Agrippa, explaining that Jesus had appeared to him on the Road to Damascus and called him to be a witness to the Gentiles, Paul said the task was "to open their eyes that they may turn from darkness to light and from the power of Satan to God" (Acts 26:18).

You are going to the secular materialist in places throughout Western Europe and the cities of the world to bring them to the lordship of Jesus Christ. You are going to the lost generations of Eastern Europe and the former Soviet Union still locked into the emptiness of their atheistic indoctrinations that they may know it is not through their humanistic efforts of self-sufficiency but the living God who brings new life. You are going to the nominal Christians of Latin America who need to know that the church and religious ritual will not save. Their eyes need to be opened so they will recognize Jesus.

How will the eyes of those who have been blinded by centuries of spiritual deception and cultural traditions be opened so they will recognize Jesus? Later the men on the road to Emmaus said, "Weren't our hearts ablaze within us while He was talking with us on the road" (Luke 24:32)? They will see the reality of Jesus as you faithfully fulfill your assignment by starting churches, discipling believers, training leaders, and contributing to the holistic ministry of your mission. They will recognize Jesus as you exhibit His indwelling presence through interpersonal relationships characterized by a love unknown in their own religious rituals. They will recognize Jesus as you reflect His grace in times of suffering, discouragement, and hardship, which are inevitable on the mission field.

Your incarnational presence should allow them to see and know Jesus through the Christlikeness they see in you. They will want to know what makes your life different. Never forget that their hearts will burn within them, and they will recognize Jesus and know Him personally only as you are faithful to verbalize your witness in a bold testimony declaring Jesus as Savior and Lord.

I have just returned from Africa, where God is moving in phenomenal ways. In the dry, dusty, impoverished country of Mali, one of our missionaries travels to the villages assisting with public health projects. The unique presence of an American in those villages enabled her to spend time telling stories in the African oral tradition—stories of God and creation, man's sin, and God's redemptive grace. Before long, the men of the villages began saying, "We want to become Christians and follow this God; we will destroy our fetishes and charms." In that isolated, primitive environment, their eyes were opened and they recognized Jesus.

Finally, I want to remind you that their eyes will be opened and they will recognize Jesus as we pray and intercede for the nations. Barriers will crumble and doors will open. Hardened hearts will become soft and responsive. God will go before those who plant their lives among the lost and bear witness to Jesus as we undergird their efforts with our prayers.

But there are still multitudes who have not had the opportunity for their eyes to be opened and recognize Jesus. Who will respond to the need for a church planter to Bangladesh, so that the 110 million Muslims of that destitute corner of the world can know Jesus? Who will go as a strategy coordinator so that the sixty-five million people of Vietnam can recognize Jesus at the time they are on the verge of restored diplomatic relations with the U.S.? Where are those who should be responding to the multitude of requests in Russia and the former Soviet republics while the door remains open? Missionary personnel have recently been assigned to eighty-five unevangelized megapeople groups with more than a million people each, but there are still 127 of these people groups with a population of more than a million untouched by the gospel. Who will say, "I will go," to the Karamonjang of Uganda, the Baluchi of Pakistan, the Mandingos of Guinea-Bissau, or the five million Makhuwa in Mozambique?

A new missionary appointee reflected that his call to missions began as a young child with the understanding that God has a special plan for all of His children. He said, "My call was to be obedient to God wherever He would lead. When I became aware of the multitude of people without Christ overseas, I could not avoid the fact that that call was to foreign missions." All of us have been called by God to give our lives to serve Him, to be a witness of the salvation He has provided in Jesus Christ. But He has given no one permission to put a geographic restriction on that call. You could be the one that has the privilege of sharing the gospel somewhere in the world with a people who need to see Jesus.

Chosen to Follow

1 Samuel 12:14–16

Samuel's challenge to the children of Israel prior to his death is an appropriate challenge to those committed to God's call to fulfill the Great Commission of our Lord. Saul had just been confirmed as king. Samuel was to have more work to do, but at this time he reminded Israel that they had been chosen of God, not unlike you have been chosen for a special task.

This prophet and priest reminded them of the consequences if they should rebel against the Lord, but I would like to focus your attention on his four words of exhortation found in 1 Samuel 12:14: "If you fear the LORD, worship and obey Him, and if you don't rebel against the LORD's command, then both you and the king who rules over you will follow the LORD your God."

1. FEAR THE LORD

Samuel begins with the basic foundation of who we are as God's people. The fear of the Lord is not something that gets much emphasis in our churches and Christian lifestyle these days.

We tend to have a greater fear for what people think of us, and the impression we make on others, than fearing the Lord. If you are normal, you probably have some fear at this moment about the immediate future, the uncertainty, the cultural transition, and language learning you will face in a foreign country; that fear is probably more prominent than the fear of God. You probably have some justifiable fear of unknown elements of the place to which you are going and fear for the health and safety of your family.

But that kind of fear will diminish in the context of an awe-inspiring fear of an Almighty God who created the heavens and the earth and controls the course of history. When you stand in daily awe, seeing the reality of His power, comprehending the scope of His eternal purpose, and experiencing the resources of His grace, you will relate to Him in a fear and respect that causes every other concern to diminish and become trivial.

As you seek the wisdom and discernment needed to bridge cultural barriers and communicate in the worldview of the people, remember, "The fear of the LORD is the beginning of wisdom" (Prov. 9:10). When you are threatened and feel insecure, remember that "the angel of the LORD encamps around those who fear Him, and rescues them" (Ps. 34:7). When you are called upon to sacrifice and have to do without some of the comforts and amenities to which you are accustomed, remember, "The eye of the LORD is on those who fear Him" (Ps. 33:18), and that the psalmist reminds us, "Those who fear Him lack nothing" (Ps. 34:9). The psalmist also reflects, "How great is Your goodness that You have stored up for those who fear You" (Ps. 31:19).

Do not forget that the first thing God called Israel to do when He announced that they were to be His special people and live the way He wanted them to live was not to serve Him, work for Him, or keep His commandments, but to fear Him. God is holy in His moral nature, His majesty, and His love. He is described as a "consuming fire" that draws us into worship whenever we contemplate Him. The vision of God's holiness and power had such a profound effect on the Old Testament saints that they came into His presence with a godly reverence and fear. That reverential fear prepares us for service and to be His witnesses in a lost world.

A. W. Tozer said, "We will be of little use to God unless we know how to tremble before Him, for otherwise our own ideas and feelings of self-sufficiency will soon take over." That is the worst thing that could happen to you on the mission field—to cease abiding in God's presence with a sense of awe and resort to your own abilities and self-sufficient efforts. The fear of God will keep your heart humble and your life faithful. It will not allow you to entertain thoughts of turning back from your divine calling. If you stand in awe of the God who called you, you will not be discouraged by obstacles, problems, or even a lack of response.

2. SERVE THE LORD

Only after establishing the fear of God as the foundation for relating to Him does Samuel say, "Serve Him." As you go to places like Japan, Korea, Brazil, Ecuador, and Chile, understand that you are not working for a mission board or serving your sending church or denomination. You are being appointed to Spain, Kenya, the Middle East, and China, not because you were enlisted and persuaded to go. Of course, your church, and the cooperative giving of your denomination will be providing your support. You will be accountable to your team of missionaries and function within certain policies, but you were called by God and are going to serve Him.

Serve Him by lifting up the name of Jesus to those who are lost, by ministering in compassion and selflessness to those who are hurting. Share the passion of missionaries who are giving themselves in ministry to Rwandan refugees, starving Somalis, or carrying the gospel to distant, isolated frontiers like Uzbekistan, and know the joy of doing it "for one of the least of these" (Matt. 25:40). Serve Jesus diligently and responsibly, whatever your assignment, whether church planting, theological education, agriculture, or logistical support. Do it unto the Lord.

3. Listen to the Lord

Then Samuel wisely says, "Listen to Him." Each of you has testified to having heard God's call. Some heard God speak to you in a seminary chapel, another in a WMU meeting or at a GA camp. Many heard God's call in the context of an overseas mission trip or through a missionary's testimony in your church. Once you hear God's call and respond, He does not get you to the mission field and then withdraw. He continues to speak and reveal His will day by day.

We have just had a furloughing missionary conference in which several confided, "I got so busy and worked so hard that I came home almost burned out. I neglected a consistent, daily time with the Lord and feel so dry and empty. I've just been going here and there, giving out and giving out without replenishing the spiritual resources that are so essential."

Do not neglect your time with the Lord. Spend time with Him every day, not just in laying your burdens and petitions before Him, but listen to Him; heed His voice. In your planning and decision making, seek His leadership and follow it. When you experience trials, family stress, and hardship, listen to Him for comfort and strength. He will speak to you and continue to reveal His heart and will. He will remind you of His promises and manifest His faithfulness.

4. FOLLOW THE LORD'S COMMANDMENTS

Finally Samuel says, "Follow His commandments." Jesus has called you to a specific task. He has called you to a certain country or people group. But primarily He has called you to obedience. There is not a circumstance or occasion in which you can justify disobedience to the Word of God. Very subtly, the enemy can cause you to rationalize and justify a rebellious spirit and cause you to assert your self-will. But the power of your testimony and the effectiveness of your witness will be a Christlike life that comes from following His commandments and allowing His presence to be manifested through you.

Dr. E. Stanley Jones told about a Hindu scholar lecturing to a group of missionaries in India. This educated Hindu said he had read the Bible and revered Christ. Then added, "If you Christians lived like Jesus, all of India would fall at your feet." As you go to share the gospel and serve in a foreign environment, let the life you live before the people be a testimony. They should see the character and holiness of Christ in the way you live because you follow His commandments and the instructions of His Word.

That will happen only as you bring your life in humble submission to God's Holy Spirit, who indwells us to guide and empower us. The fleshly power of our sinful nature will assure certain failure if we ever presume to obey God's commandments in our own strength and efforts. We cannot obey because we ought to or out of a sense of obligation. Obedience will come only as we fear Him, listen to Him, and serve Him in the power of His Spirit. And the testimony of a Christlike life gives credibility to our verbal witness.

After Samuel challenged Israel to (1) fear the Lord, (2) serve the Lord, (3) listen to His voice, and (4) obey His commandments, he then said, "Now, therefore, present yourselves and see this great thing that the LORD will do before your eyes" (1 Sam. 12:16). All over the world, we are seeing the Lord move in unprecedented ways. Doors of opportunity are opening as never before. Churches are being started in unlikely places such as Mongolia and Albania. A miraculous harvest is being reaped among the Maasai in Africa, and people are being saved among the Fulani, Kanuri, and other unreached people groups for the first time. As one missionary exclaimed during my recent trip to Africa, "The gospel is not just a message; it is something that is happening."

As you walk in fear of the Lord, are faithful to serve Him, to listen to Him and obey Him, I assure you that you will see Him going before you to manifest His power and extend His kingdom. Some would look with pity on you for having been chosen to leave the comfortable life and amenities of America, but you are the ones who have the privilege of taking the life-transforming message of the gospel to a lost world. You have the honor to be chosen to make a difference in a world suffering and in despair. As you go in obedience to the Great Commission, the Lord will do great things before your eyes.

But there is a bonus. Later in this chapter as Samuel finished his challenge, he is recorded as saying, "As for me, I vow that I will not sin against the Lord by ceasing to pray for you" (1 Sam. 12:23). As you go, be assured of the prayers of God's people for you. We are partners with you as you fear the Lord, listen to Him, serve Him, and obey His commandments.

4

Don't Stop Short ♫

2 Kings 2:1–15

With each service of commissioning new missionaries to go in obedience to the Great Commission, I recall my own experience of being affirmed and sent out. It was something to which I had looked forward to for many years, for God had called me at a very young age. It was a thrilling and inspirational moment to finally take that obedient step in going to the mission field. I went back to our little community in north Texas after that appointment service for the final weeks of ministry before departure for orientation, and I could not understand what was happening. I did not feel the overwhelming joy and excitement that I thought I would feel. There was no question about God's call; I had no doubts there. I had no anxiety about what I faced in living overseas because I was confident this was God's will for my life. But I could not understand why the thrill and anticipation I expected to accompany this step of obedience was missing.

As I turned to the Lord and prayed, it seemed that God spoke to me in a very convicting way. I realized that I was going to Indonesia with the same spiritual mediocrity that I had here in America, and I knew it was not enough! That conviction placed in my heart a desire that I feel was expressed by Elisha in the Bible, just before he embarked upon his appointed mission. Elisha had spent a time of apprenticeship following Elijah. In 2 Kings 2:9, before Elijah relinquished his ministry to Elisha, he asked—possibly as God would ask you at this time—"What would you like me to do with you before you go to the mission field, before you assume that responsibility?" Elisha knew exactly what he wanted. He said, "Please, let there be a double portion of your spirit on me." He recognized at that point his own inadequacy and his need. If he was to fulfill his appointed mission, he didn't need what Elijah had, but he needed twice as much!

Before we went to Indonesia, like Elisha, God placed in my heart a burning desire for nothing less than an outpouring of God's Spirit, for I realized how inadequate I was for the task to which He had called me. Elijah replied in response to this request, "You've asked a hard thing." Not that it is hard for the Lord, or something that God did not want to give to him, but I think what Elijah meant was that it is not easy to receive that kind of filling of God's Spirit. And he said to him, "You've got to go all the way; you can't stop short if that's what you want."

Elijah must have realized what Elisha would ask for. For remember, as they were going along the way, in the earlier verses of 2 Kings 2, before Elijah was taken from him, they came to various places on the journey, and Elisha was tempted to stop along the way. You, too, will go to the mission field; you will be obedient to God's call and take your family to live and work overseas. But you will be tempted to stop short of going all the way in the discipline and focused commitment that are required to receive the anointing and blessing of God's power.

First, don't stop at Gilgal. The first place they came to was Gilgal, and Elijah said, "Stay here; the LORD is sending me on to Bethel" (v. 2). But Elisha replied, "No, I'm not going to stay here. As the Lord lives and as you live, I'm going all the way. I'm going with you." In Hebrew, the word *Gilgal* means "circle" or "wheel." I would like to suggest that many who would desire to go all the way with an infilling of God's Spirit and empowering have stopped at Gilgal.

Someone from East Africa told me that the word for "foreigner" in Swahili was *wazunggu*, which comes from a word that means to go around in circles. What an indictment on us as Americans, as foreigners, that we would be seen as those who are so busy and active that we appear to be going around in circles and yet never getting anywhere. You will find that there is the temptation to substitute busyness and activities for the fullness of God's Spirit. You will find your time consumed with keeping the children cheerful, the family fed, the helpers happy, the pastors appeased. There will be so many demands on your time that you will likely realize you are accomplishing little for the Lord. You will need more than a strong work ethic and lengthy to-do list. Staying busy with programs and activities doesn't necessarily get the job done. If you want an outpouring of God's Spirit and power, you cannot stop at Gilgal and be satisfied with staying busy and going around in circles. Elisha would not stop there, so they went on to Bethel.

Second, don't stop at Bethel. You know what Bethel means— the house of God. You would think that is the place where one would find an outpouring of God's Spirit. After all, the church is the objective of your ministry. God is calling you to lead people to salvation and to plant churches that become a nucleus of indigenous, local witness. But like so many in America, you can very subtly find yourself caught up in the programs, the commitments, the time-consuming tasks and functions of the church without any evidence of a spiritual movement of God. The life, the vitality, and the evidence of God's power are lacking. Often one substitutes the assignment of church planting for what is really needed and fails to go all the way in receiving what is needed from God.

My wife once chided me for how I described our best members when engaged in pastoring a church. I would describe them as "faithful and active." They may never witness to their neighbors, and their lives might not reflect Christlike character, but they were faithful to attend church—always there when the doors were open! Just being faithful, even in church-related programs and activities, is not the same as a Spirit-filled life of power. Teaching at a seminary, taking care of business affairs, doing agricultural work, health-care work, even planting churches can become a substitute for the outpouring power of God that is necessary to draw a lost world to Christ. Do not stop at Bethel. Carry out your assignment faithfully, serve the church, but do not substitute methodology and church-planting strategy for going all the way to receive God's filling and power.

Third, don't stop at Jericho. Elisha did not stop at Bethel, but he accompanied Elijah in going down to Jericho, the next town on their journey. The name *Jericho* means "fragrance" or "luxury." It refers to a place of gardens. You will find it tempting to become focused on the comforts of your lifestyle once you arrive overseas. Probably, at this point, you are more committed and ready to sacrifice whatever the assignment calls for in terms of personal comfort than you may ever be again. However, once you get on the field in the heat of the tropics, in the midst of congested masses of people, and are confronted with the lack of amenities you have taken for granted in America, your attitude will change, and the complaining will begin. As you begin to fix up your house and engage in a time-consuming search through the market for Diet Coke, it is easy to forget that the call of God was a call to die to self and to surrender all to Him.

I will never forget being in an annual meeting of missionaries as we discussed with great conviction the matter of lifestyle; it was evident God was moving in our hearts. We were talking about moving down to a lower profile and giving up some of the luxuries of our lifestyle in order to identify more closely with the people with whom we worked. We were genuinely convicted concerning the inappropriateness of our large houses and pretentious lifestyles. One of the women stood up and said tearfully, "I agree with the decisions we are making, but I just can't give up my refrigerator!" I have often thought about that, as there are missionaries in places where there is no electricity and who do not have a refrigerator. However, at the time I thought God probably did not want us to give up her refrigerator. He knows our needs and wants us to provide for sanitation and the health of our families. But we better be willing to give up having a refrigerator or anything else if that is what being obedient to God's call entails. One cannot hold on to a sense of entitlement and fulfill God's calling in the power of His Spirit. Elisha refused to be diverted by a comfortable lifestyle and stop at Jericho, so with Elijah he went on to the Jordan River.

Fourth, don't stop at the Jordan River. *Jordan* means "descender," as it flows down a rift valley from the Sea of Galilee to the Dead Sea far below sea level. I would just suggest that the Jordan represents anything in your life that pulls you down to a level less than what God wants you to be. You may not stop at Gilgal and be satisfied with busyness and activity in your missionary service. You may not stop at Bethel and substitute just serving church programs. You may not stop at Jericho and be diverted by concerns about lifestyle and comforts. But is there anything in your life keeping God from pouring out His spirit in all of His fullness and power?

Perhaps you carry a root of bitterness and an unforgiving spirit, a spirit of anger, low self-esteem, problems in relationships, maybe a besetting sin, or a spirit of pride of having arrived now that you are a missionary. Whatever it is, you have got to deal with it, resolve it, and cross over to the other side to receive the outpouring of God's power. Elisha received that double portion of God's Spirit because he was willing to go all the way and not stop short. He was not satisfied with any substitute because his passionate desire was the fullness of God's anointing.

When the spirit of Elijah fell upon him, Elisha tore off his robe—that which symbolized a covering of self-righteousness and self-sufficiency. There was nothing left of self-confidence in his own ability. As he went back, he came to the Jordan River again, and there the waters were flowing as they had before; the time of testing came. Had he received what he asked for? Had God anointed him and empowered him with the spirit of Elijah for his ministry? He took the mantle of Elijah, struck the waters, and said, "Where is the LORD God of Elijah?" The waters parted, and he went across to the other side.

It will not be long before testing will come—when you encounter the challenge of language learning and adjusting to life cross-culturally, or when your children are ill and there is no adequate medical care available. You will receive news from home of family needs and feel so far away and helpless. When you encounter challenges and opposition to your witness, you will find yourself saying, "Where is the Lord God of Elijah?" Will you see the power of God because you have gone all the way in your surrender? It is not enough just to be here saying, "I am available; I'm willing to go overseas to be a missionary." It is not enough to make a geographic move and go to a foreign country; you need to go all the way in dying to self, surrendering your life, and opening your heart to receive the Spirit and empowering of God that is available. The condition is to go all the way.

What enabled Elisha to go all the way? We need to go back to 1 Kings 19, when Elijah first found him plowing in the field and cast his mantle upon him signifying the call to come and follow as an apprentice prophet. Elisha started to go after him, then he turned back and killed his oxen; he took the plow implements, made an altar, and sacrificed them to the Lord. Then he went and followed Elijah. In other words, he burned his bridges behind him. There was nothing to go back to. He was committed to going all the way. I pray that you will burn your bridges behind you as you go in obedience to God's call. Say, "I am not looking back. I am not holding on to the past and all that I am leaving. I'm not going to stop at Gilgal or Bethel or Jericho or the Jordan and be satisfied with less than God's power and anointing. I am committed to go all the way."

5

Learning God's Lessons

Psalm 143:6–10

Each commissioning of new missionaries is an emotional experience for me as I recall my own appointment as a new missionary. This service at Ridgecrest Baptist Assembly is especially nostalgic, for it was here during a Foreign Mission Week twenty-five years ago that my family and I were appointed for service in Indonesia. In addition to us, there were couples going to Uganda, Guatemala, Korea, the Philippines, Liberia, and two families who were assigned to open Southern Baptist work in Laos. For some reason, we were asked to sing a contemporary missions song in closing. I don't know why—we aren't uniquely qualified as vocalists. In fact, I remember someone suggesting I stand away from the microphones! I don't know that I have ever seen that done again. After a stirring challenge by Dr. Baker James Cauthen, then president of the Foreign Mission Board, we sang the song "Here Is My Life," a contemporary song of commitment by Ed Seabough and Gene Bartlett.

There were only sixteen of us in that 1970 appointment service. Now an appointment group of seventy to eighty new missionaries is not uncommon as record numbers surrender to the challenge of Great Commission obedience. It was amazing to us that, in the midst of the war in Indochina in 1970, Southern Baptist missionaries would be going to Laos. Not in our wildest imagination would we have dreamed that today we would be sending you to places such as Uzbekistan, Russia, Moldova, Romania, and Lithuania. It was beyond our most visionary plans and strategies that others of you would be going to join in such an amazing harvest of souls as we are seeing in Africa and Latin America today.

Like others being appointed, we had responded many years before to a call to missions. We had finally completed the education and practical experience required in the appointment process. Our adrenalin was flowing, and we were ready to get to the field. But we found that we were ill prepared for the journey of faith, the cross-cultural adjustments, and spiritual warfare which we would face for the next twenty-three years. Our initial term was a learning experience in which God taught us lessons essential not only to success but to survival on the mission field.

We could identify with the psalmist who longed to see God's power manifested in his life but realized what was lacking was no deficiency on God's part. It was his own need to be taught and to learn to trust the Lord. "I spread out my hands to You; I am like parched land before You. Answer me quickly, Lord; my spirit fails. Don't hide Your face from me, or I will be like those going down to the Pit. Let me experience Your faithful love in the morning, for I trust in You. Reveal to me the way I should go, because I long for You. . . . Teach me to do Your will, for You are my God" (Ps. 143:6–8, 10). You need to go with a teachable spirit, acknowledging there are lessons you need to learn in order to be effective and to persevere in fulfilling God's will. Among the things God taught us during our first term was the reliability of His Word, the reality of His power, and the resources of His grace.

THE RELIABILITY OF GOD'S WORD

The first lesson we discovered was the reliability of God's Word. We truly believed that the Bible was God's inspired, infallible Word, but we found God's promises to be true and His word to be dependable when we had nothing else to which to cling.

During my first term I had found a pocket of response in a rural Muslim village and had been meeting with them for several weeks. As their growing interest confirmed the convicting work of God's Spirit, I had given them Bibles and encouraged them to read them. They did so with eagerness, and each time I met with them, they would have many questions. I recall someone asking a difficult question about an obscure passage. As I heard myself explain that it was necessary to understand the historical background and the context of the original language, I saw their demeanor change, and God immediately checked my response. I was communicating to these spiritually hungry, barely literate new believers that they really couldn't understand God's Word without a great deal of education and sophisticated knowledge.

From that day the focus of my ministry, and indeed my life, began to change. I was in Indonesia to bear witness to a living Savior, but having led people to Jesus Christ, my passion was to put in their hands the living Word of God and teach them to read it and to believe and practice whatever they read. I could not always be there to explain it and to teach them. Their growth in faith and functioning as a church could not be dependent on my leadership but on the truth and reliability of God's Word.

An amazing thing began to happen! I began to see these new congregations growing in faith and boldness, praying with fervor, reminding God what He had said, and then believing Him to bring it about. I watched as they functioned as a fellowship of believers with multiple, gifted leadership as a church ought to function. I saw them reach out in ministry to neighbors who were suffering because that's what God's Word taught them to do. I saw them pray for a miracle to end a drought, or for healing for those who were sick, and then rejoice as God did just what He said He would do.

I tried to mess it up occasionally! I had been meeting with a new church group on Tuesday evening and tried to persuade them to begin gathering and worshipping on Sunday; since it was the day of Christian worship, it would be a testimony to their Muslim village. In response they explained they were already meeting on Sunday . . . and on Monday, Tuesday, Wednesday, Thursday, Friday, and Saturday. They had read in Acts 5:42 that the believers were "every day in the temple complex, and in various homes, they continued teaching and proclaiming . . . Jesus." They asked if they should stop doing that and only meet on Sunday now that they were a church. I realized my tendency to teach from my own traditions and interpretations instead of the purity of God's Word and began to discover how dependable God's Word was in my own life.

You will encounter many anxious situations but will discover the truth of God's Word which says, "The peace of God, which surpasses every thought, will guard your hearts and your minds in Christ Jesus" (Phil. 4:7). God's Word is reliable. Many of you are going to places that are resistant to the gospel. Remember, as you encounter obstacles and rejection and doubts begin to fill your mind, that God's Word says, "The earth will be filled with the knowledge of the LORD's glory, as the waters cover the sea" (Hab. 2:14).

THE REALITY OF GOD'S POWER

Another lesson we learned quickly on the mission field was the reality of God's power. If you haven't recognized it already, you will quickly discover that God hasn't called you because of your training and abilities but because He considers you a worthy channel of His Spirit and power. Certainly He will use your education and equipping; He has given you talents and gifts, but He also said, "You will receive power when the Holy Spirit has come upon you, and you will be My witnesses" (Acts 1:8). You, too, will learn the reality of God's power in the diverse places you are going as you are faithful to lift up Jesus Christ in your witness.

I am still amazed when I think of Muslims coming to faith in Christ. It defies explanation, for they would often be rejected by their families, lose their jobs, be ridiculed in their communities; sometimes their lives would be threatened. Why would they turn their backs on their culture, religion, and society to embrace a faith introduced by a foreigner? It was not because of our wisdom and persuasive words, trying to communicate in a language that was not natural. The only explanation is the power of God that indwells the message of the gospel. Remember as you go that "the gospel . . . is God's power for salvation to everyone who believes, first to the Jew, and also to the Greek" (Rom. 1:16).

In 1977 the Department of Religion in Indonesia said that missionaries could stay no longer than three years in the country. As we prayed, I happened to read Psalm 47:8, which says, "God reigns over the nations; God is seated on His holy throne," and a few weeks later the head of the religion department was changed, and that law was never implemented! The reality of God's power will be evident as He opens closed doors, as He stays the hand of Pharaoh, and as He manifests His power in signs and wonders that Christ might be lifted up and glorified.

Our prayer for you tonight is that which was prayed by Paul for the believers at Ephesus, "That [God] may grant you, according to the riches of His glory, to be strengthened with power through His Spirit in the inner man" (Eph. 3.16).

The Resources of God's Grace

Finally, in addition to the reliability of God's Word and the reality of God's power, it is essential you learn the resources of God's grace. As John closed his Gospel and reflected on the life of Jesus, he said the world could not contain the books if all were written of what Jesus did and said. Neither could the world contain the testimonies of God's grace in the lives of missionaries around the world if they were to all be written down. You have the privilege of experiencing those resources as you follow His leadership to strange and distant places.

In the last few months we have had the privilege of traveling to China and East Asia, Romania, and throughout South America. We met missionaries who live in remote locations without conveniences and social outlets they had thought were so essential, but in every situation they testified to finding God's grace sufficient. We were with families experiencing debilitating illnesses or grieving over the loss of a parent far away in the States, but they shared how God had manifested His precious grace beyond what they had ever known before.

My family and I have not had experiences nearly as difficult as many others, but early in our tenure overseas God taught us about the resources of His grace. We had just finished language study and had begun our assignment in a location hours away from any of our missionary colleagues. We had been fighting staphylococcus infections breaking out all over our bodies, probably from our water supply. As we were eating dinner one night, we happened to notice that a boil on our two-year-old son's forehead was enlarged, and a red streak extended down to his eye. Sensing intuitively the danger of the infection draining into his brain, we left our food on the table and left for our Baptist hospital, five hours away. When we got there about midnight, both of his eyes were swollen shut, and they told us later, after pumping him with antibiotics, that we would have lost him if we had not come that night. Since we were at the hospital, we all got a checkup and found that Bobbye, my wife, needed major surgery. That delayed our return home, but we did get back a couple of weeks before Christmas, only for both of us to come down with dengue fever. There is nothing you can do about dengue fever other than let it run its course; it is sometimes called "breakbone fever" because you feel that your head and every bone in your body are breaking.

That was a miserable Christmas—alone, far away from family and friends, wallowing in bed with a burning fever, Bobbye still recovering from surgery, and having almost lost our son. Then the day after Christmas the phone rang; it was a call from the States informing us that Bobbye's parents had been in an automobile accident. Her father had been killed, and her mother was in critical condition. Never had we felt so helpless and alone. We held each other and cried. Other missionaries were notified and soon arrived to comfort and care for us. But in the midst of that time of trial, God revealed Himself to us; we experienced the presence of Jesus and an outpouring of God's grace that we had never known before.

As you go to fulfill the challenge of the Great Commission, don't assume that God is going to protect you from harm, deflect hardship and difficulty, and thwart every trial. You will have an opportunity to discover, as Paul did when God did not remove his thorn in the flesh, that "My grace is sufficient for you, for power is perfected in weakness." Your reply should be as Paul's as you learn these lessons, "I will most gladly boast all the more about my weaknesses, so that Christ's power may reside in me" (2 Cor. 12:9).

God has many lessons to teach you as you go to the field in obedience to His call. You are well prepared and qualified but still have a lot to learn. May you quickly discover the reliability of God's Word, the reality of God's power, and the resources of God's grace.

6

Go with a Broken Heart

Psalm 126:5–6

Each morning before spending an extended time in prayer and systematic Bible study, I begin my devotional time with a cup of coffee and reading in the Psalms. The Psalms seem to put the challenges of the day in perspective as I capture a sense of God's greatness and my heart is lifted in praise. Recently, I was deeply impressed that a familiar passage reflected a critical focus of the missionary task. "Those who sow in tears will reap with shouts of joy. Though one goes along weeping, carrying the bag of seed, he will surely come back with shouts of joy, carrying his sheaves" (Ps. 126:5–6).

This is why you are being appointed in obedience to the Great Commission of our Lord. It is the reason God called you to leave the familiarity of this country, your family and church fellowship, to go to a foreign country. You are to sow the seed of the gospel and experience the joy of reaping the harvest in the fields of the world.

Each of you has testified of an experience of coming to know Christ as your personal Lord and Savior. At some point in your life, someone told you about Jesus. Your salvation may have come at an early age as a natural result of church involvement or because of concerned Christian parents. For others, it was later as a teenager or as a young adult when a friend cared enough to speak to you about Christ. It may have been in a timely moment of God's providence when you attended a revival service and the claims of Jesus on your life became clear. It is not unusual that some of you conformed to expectations to join the church and be baptized, only to discover later the reality of knowing Jesus in an experience of being born again. Whatever the timing and circumstances of knowing God, you began to be impressed with His call to share that experience in places where people did not know Him. You are being commissioned to sow the seed of the gospel in assignments throughout the world.

I can personally recall many events, experiences, and impressions which could be interpreted as a call to missions, but I invariably find myself all the way back to my salvation experience as a ten-year-old boy. I had known about Jesus all my life, but in one particular timely church service, I came under the conviction of sin and realized I was separated from God. As I opened my heart and prayed to receive Christ as Savior, I was filled with a sense of peace and joy in knowing I had entered into a personal relationship with God that was eternally secure. I can still recall the distinct impression of wishing everyone in the world could know that same joy and peace that comes with knowing Jesus.

A call to missions and obedience to Christ's command to make disciples of all nations should be inherent in one's salvation experience. That is because those without faith in Jesus Christ are lost and bound for an eternity of separation from God. And it is also because those of us who have had an opportunity to hear and respond to the gospel have a responsibility to share it with others. The apostle Paul described it as a debt we owe to those who are lost: "I am obligated both to Greeks and barbarians, both to the wise and the foolish. So I am eager to preach the good news to you also" (Rom. 1:14–15).

You would not be going to the mission field if you did not have that same sense of obligation to proclaim the gospel. Such a compelling obligation is due to the conviction that those who do not believe on Jesus Christ are lost and under condemnation for sin. But you are also going in obedience to God's call because you believe God can use you to bring them to salvation as you faithfully sow the seed and bear witness to God's love.

I discovered a valuable, foundational principle upon arrival on the mission field; it is the fact that wherever Jesus is lifted up in a bold, positive witness, people will be saved—not everyone, as there will always be those with hardened hearts who will reject the message. But it is simply the nature of the gospel, the purpose of God, and the power of the Holy Spirit which indwells that message, for it to draw people to faith in Jesus Christ when it is clearly and boldly proclaimed.

Some of you are going to serve in remote and primitive locations in Africa. Others are going to live among the most densely populated areas of the world in Asia. There are those of you going to sophisticated cultures of Europe or to the Catholic-dominated societies of Latin America. Some will find open doors and ready response while others will be impacting people groups that remain relatively closed and inaccessible.

SOW THE GOSPEL WITH A BROKEN HEART

Whatever the context of your ministry, whatever the nature of your assignment, allow this passage in Psalms to speak to you. You will never reap the harvest and be successful in bringing redeemed souls into the kingdom if your heart ever ceases to be broken over the lostness of people without Jesus. Only those who sow in tears—

brokenhearted over the lostness of the people around them—will have the longing, the desire, the passion to persist in witness and introduce them to the Savior. Only as you carry the precious seed of the gospel, weeping over those who have never known God's mercy and love, will you have a motivating compulsion that will result in people being saved.

You will be overwhelmed with the multitudes crowded into the bazaars and marketplaces, but never forget they are lost. As you get caught in the snarl of traffic of honking cars entangled with bicycles, motorcycles, oxcarts, and pedestrians, remember these people are lost.

As you see the smoke rising from African villages or observe the towering skyscrapers in the great urban centers of the world, realize they represent people who are lost. As you survey the endless factories emerging in global industrialization, be reminded they represent multitudes of individuals still in bondage to sin. When you register in government offices, go to buy groceries or pick up your mail at the post office, recognize that the people you encounter are lost.

Don't forget the importance of what the psalmist is saying. One of the quickest things that will happen in your adjustment to the mission field is the loss of a broken heart. You will still have a burden to reach the lost; you can't forget why you are there as you see so many people who do not know God. But you will get caught up with your own needs—providing for the comforts of your home and family. You will find your time being diverted to things that bring personal fulfillment and enjoyment. The crowds and traffic will become an inconvenience and irritant, instead of a reminder of people who are lost that will break your heart.

It is not unlikely that you will grow suspicious of the people, fearing they will rob you, cheat you, or harm you. Instead of a broken heart, you will find your heart becoming hardened, and instead of reaching out, you will withdraw; instead of loving, you will find yourself resenting. I confess that I allowed a cynicism to develop soon after our arrival in Indonesia. People would come and express an interest in becoming a Christian. But after talking with them and leading them in a prayer of commitment, invariably they would ask for money or a job or if I would sponsor them to go to America. I can assure you that people will take advantage of you; they will use you; they will want to borrow money and will want you to teach them English. But guard your heart against skepticism. Don't be entrapped by questioning motives that would cause you to ignore a genuine inquirer. You can easily find your heart becoming calloused and the tears ceasing to flow as you look into the faces of people who are lost.

Each day in Indonesia I would be awakened at 4:30 a.m. by the irritating, discordant chant from the nearby mosque calling the people to prayer as the sound of the loudspeakers reverberated throughout the neighborhood. Initially I was angry that this irritating religious ritual disturbed my right to sound sleep. But something began to happen each time I heard this call to prayer five times a day. My heart became heavy as it reminded me that the people in this Muslim culture responding to that call to prayer were being deceived and led astray. My heart was broken as I was reminded of their lostness, and my zeal was renewed to sow the seed and introduce them to Jesus.

I'll never forget one of our field leaders in East Africa telling about a volunteer assisting with relief efforts in Somalia. The truck they were using in the feeding program had a machine gun mounted on the cab. Due to the anarchy and warfare going on about them, they were always accompanied by armed guards. A young boy approached the feeding station, and the guard ordered him to put down a weapon he was carrying; instead he lifted his rifle to his shoulder, and the guard shot him on the spot. The volunteer—a big, stocky man—broke down and cried. When the guard asked him why he was crying, that he didn't know the boy and his life had just been saved and people were being killed all around them, he replied, "But I didn't have a chance to tell him about Jesus."

Don't ever cease seeing the people around you as God sees them. Look at the people you pass on the street—your neighbors, the immigration and customs officials you encounter when you enter the country—and see persons, individuals whom God loves. Think, "Here is a person for whom Christ died." Remind yourself why you are there; it is because people are lost and someone needs to sow the seed. They are alienated from God, without hope, bound for a Christless eternity. They are missing the joy of a new life and the victory which you are privileged to experience—not because they don't want to be saved or because they have rejected Jesus Christ but because no one has ever told them. You are called to go and sow the seed of the gospel; do it with a broken heart. Only as you sow in tears will you have the joy of seeing response.

REAP THE HARVEST WITH JOY

The greatest joy I have ever experienced, even greater than my own salvation, is seeing someone who has never heard of Jesus and never comprehended the love of God to respond to my witness and be saved. You will reap with joy; you will bear sheaves into the kingdom—precious souls who have found Jesus—as you go with tears, weeping and broken for a lost world.

God has assured us of the harvest if we maintain a broken heart. How do we keep from becoming calloused and indifferent? It comes from spending time with God and knowing His heart, a heart that is broken over those for whom He died that do not yet know Him as Savior and Lord. The psalmist reminds us: "Stop [your fighting]— and know that I am God, exalted among the nations, exalted on the earth" (Ps. 46:10).

God will be exalted among the nations. Hold to that promise; let the vision of all peoples praising and worshipping God compel you in your witness and enable you to persevere. But recognize the prerequisite condition for seeing that happen is to be still and know God. You have to turn aside from the busy, hectic pace of life; you have got to stop trying to work harder and accomplish more through your own efforts and spend time with Him.

You are probably at a peak of commitment and resolve as you are commissioned to go in response to a call to a lost world. But you will soon be caught up in packing, travel, language learning, and other demands on your time. You are likely to be overcome by fatigue and weariness and will begin to neglect your time with God. I pray you will be constantly reminded of your own inadequacy and will be driven to depend wholly on the Lord. Your intimate personal relationship with Him will keep your heart broken for a lost world. And your broken heart will keep you sowing the seed of the gospel with tears. When your heart is in tune with God's, the tears will flow, but you will be able to rejoice in bringing lost souls into the kingdom. Go with a broken heart, sow in tears, and reap the harvest with joy.

7

The Call of Abraham

Genesis 12:1–2

Being commissioned to overseas service is the culmination of a process in which God has worked in your life and revealed a personal call. For some, it was the result of overseas travel to places where you have seen the needs of a lost world and seen God at work. A time of orientation and training will be needed in preparation for the task on the field where you are going to serve. In fact, you have probably thought of becoming a missionary fairly exclusively in terms of going, for Jesus said, "Go into all the world and preach the gospel to the whole creation" (Mark 16:15). He said, "Go, therefore, and make disciples of all nations" (Matt. 28:19). But response to God's call is more than going; it is also a call to leave and a call to follow.

THE CALL TO GO IS A CALL TO LEAVE

When God called Abraham, He said, "Go out from your land, your relatives, and your father's house" (Gen. 12:1). The foundational aspect of Abraham's call was not in launching out on an adventurous journey or a call to a destination—the promised land. It was a call to leave. He would never have gotten to the place and the role to which God was calling Him had he not been willing to leave his native country and to leave his father and relatives. You may be from a close family and feel tied to your parents, but it was nothing like the bonding of a Middle Eastern family in the time of Abraham. It was unthinkable that a son would leave his father, whom he was obligated to serve. But such was the call of Abraham, just as it is yours.

This summer I have heard in a number of mission conferences a testimony by a young lady serving in Shanghai, China, a sprawling city of fourteen million people. She described this ancient port city in the most graphic terms of teeming masses of humanity, inadequate sanitation, traffic snarls, and crowded markets; then she paused and added, "And I love it!"

She is a teacher who has given herself to the students and people of Shanghai. She loves it because she is called there. But she could never love it and plant her life in such circumstances if she had not been called to leave the successful and fulfilling ministry and job security she had in the States. She had to be willing to leave her family and friends and the comforts and amenities she had in America.

Wherever we travel overseas, my wife, Bobbye, often asks missionaries the question, "Are you feeling at home here?" Sometimes newer ones will equivocate and say something to the effect, "We're getting there," but almost without exception others will say, "Yes, this is home." That is evident when missionaries come home on furlough. Stateside families cannot understand that after visiting awhile, going to a few ball games and shopping at Walmart, the kids will start saying, "Daddy, when are we going home to Brazil, to Malawi, or to Korea?"

But the place to which you are called overseas doesn't become home unless you recognize that a call to go is also a call to leave. You will never truly identify with the people and be effective in your witness and ministry until you let go of what you have left behind. That means missing birthdays, class reunions, and significant family events. You cannot always be with loved ones to minister in times of need, and that's difficult for your parents and family. They need to understand that God's grace is sufficient for them as well. There is a special blessing for those of you who are willing to give of your sons and daughters and be deprived of quality time with your grandchildren in order for them to be obedient to God's call.

THE CALL TO GO IS A CALL TO FOLLOW

Becoming a missionary implies a special relationship with your heavenly Father. You have responded, not just to a call to go to a specific place, though you are being appointed to a certain field and a specific job assignment; but you are going in submission to the lordship of Jesus Christ. That means a commitment to follow, even though it may imply uncertainty as you face the unknown.

The Scripture says of Abraham's call, "By faith Abraham, when he was called, obeyed and went out to a place he was going to receive as an inheritance; he went out, not knowing where he was going" (Heb. 11:8). That would be difficult, wouldn't it? What if we said to each of you, "We are appointing you tonight because you have said you will go wherever God leads. We don't know where you will be sent, and a little later we are going to place in your hand an airline ticket; you won't know the destination or what you are going to encounter when you get there." That's what Abraham experienced, and he was obedient.

You know where God is leading you—for now. In fact, you have probably already read and studied a great deal about the country and talked to missionaries and staff about what you will do there, but no one can guarantee the future. Missionaries in half a dozen countries this year have been told by the government that their visas and work permits would not be extended. Some have successfully appealed, but others have had to transfer to another field. Dozens of missionaries are evacuated from time to time because of war or escalating violence. How do you reconcile that with the call of God that told you to go to that field?

I recall one of our missionaries being called to a restricted field but unable to get a visa. He and his family traveled in and out of the country on tourist visas, exploring various platforms and serving in interim assignments in nearby countries. After a year and a half, they were finally granted a work permit and able to locate on a new field where people had never heard the gospel. But during those eighteen months, they had lived in fifteen different places—not a very convenient lifestyle for a family with three small children. I will never forget their testimony as they were leaving to assume their assignment. They said, "We never knew where we would be from one month to the next; however, one thing God has taught us through this experience is that He calls not so much to a place but to Himself."

When we respond to that call—a call to the lordship of Christ—it doesn't really matter where we are. God's call is not just a call to a place; it is a call to follow wherever He leads. God's call is not just to a country or a location; it is not a call to an unchanging assignment. It is not a call just to be a missionary. It is a call to follow in obedience day by day. God knows the circumstances you will face, some which will appear to be obstacles to your understanding of God's will. You will not always know how things are going to work out; your call is to trust God and follow Him in obedience.

The Call to Go Is Accompanied By a Promise

Not only is the call to go a call to leave and a call to follow; it is also a call with a promise. God said to Abraham, "I will make you into a great nation, I will bless you, I will make your name great" (Gen. 12:2). God gave assurance to Abraham of His blessings, but receiving God's blessings was contingent on Abraham's being obedient and responding to God's call.

As you go in obedience to God's call, I can assure you that you will face times of loneliness and self-pity when you miss your family and feel deprived. I have heard of missionaries complaining because they could not get Dr Pepper or Diet Coke in the country where they lived. Our true values seem to surface when something really does have to be sacrificed for the sake of the call. God does not promise material blessings and comforts, but He does promise blessings that are far superior to anything of that nature. He has said that He will provide for your needs, but those needs are usually far less than you would ever imagine. God will bless you with the joy of knowing Him in His fullness that only comes with obedience. He will give you joy and fulfillment that come from giving one's self in service for others. I can assure you that there is no greater blessing than having the privilege of introducing someone to Jesus Christ who has never before heard of Him!

I believe God would say to you, as He promised Abraham, "I will bless you, I will make your name great" (Gen. 12:2), because you have responded to My call to go, My call to leave, and My call to follow. And that is all that is important. It is not your reputation or being great in the eyes of others; greatest in God's eyes is being an obedient servant. But a second promise is associated with obedience to God's call. In Genesis 12:2–3, God says, "And you will be a blessing. . . . and all the peoples on earth will be blessed."

God has called you to missionary service, not for yourself, but for others. His purpose is for repentance and forgiveness of sins to be proclaimed to all nations—among the *panta ta ethne*—all peoples of the world. God's desire is not just to bless you, but His call to you is so that all peoples might be blessed by receiving the redemption He has provided through Jesus Christ.

It is unfortunate that so many Christians see their salvation as something for their own benefit. God did not save us just to keep us out of hell. How arrogant that we would think God would show us such favor just for ourselves. You have recognized that God has saved you for a purpose—the purpose of sharing Him with others. If we are blessed with the privilege of knowing Jesus Christ, it is because, as the psalmist proclaimed, "that Your way may be known on earth, Your salvation among all nations" (67:2)!

We know that God's purpose will be fulfilled as one day there will be "a vast multitude from every nation, tribe, people, and language, . . . standing before the throne and before the Lamb" (Rev. 7:9). God is breaking down barriers and opening doors of opportunity so the gospel can be proclaimed for the first time among unreached people groups to which many of you are being assigned. He is moving across Eastern Europe and former communist countries so long deprived of the freedom of religion and accelerating the harvest in Asia, Africa, and Latin America.

He is promising you, that because you go, "you will be a blessing," and through you and your witness "all the families of the earth will be blessed" because they have the opportunity to know Jesus and become a part of God's eternal kingdom being extended throughout the world.

Many others should be joining you. They haven't responded to God's call to go because they are unwilling to leave, they are unwilling to follow, and they do not comprehend the blessings of obedience which God has promised to those who go.

8

Equipping for the Task

Proverbs 8:14

Some of you being appointed tonight have responded to a call to missions that was quite sudden and recent, but for others, your appointment is the culmination of a lengthy process that perhaps began even as a child. God spoke to you as an RA or GA or as a young person. He continued to confirm that profound impression until you knew beyond a shadow of a doubt that God was calling you into missions. You may have resisted or been diverted in another direction, but you have come to the point of being commissioned in obedience to that call.

My own call to missions came soon after my salvation experience. In my preteens, I had been discipled to understand that God had a plan and purpose for my life, and missions came into focus very early. For many years, throughout high school, college, seminary, and pastoral experience, I saw everything as preparation for the mission field. I took mission courses in seminary, participated in summer missions overseas, and learned everything I could from the missionaries I met. Finally, after appointment, a fourteen-week orientation, and an initial year of language study, we moved to our place of assignment in Jember, Indonesia. I don't think I could adequately describe the awesome feeling and the frightening emotions of that experience. All at once we were there! What do you do? No more preparation. No more waiting, study, and training. My wife, Bobbye, and I found ourselves with two small children, isolated as the only foreigners in the midst of 5.5 million people on the eastern tip of Java, wondering, *What do we do now?*

In a few months you are going to experience something similar to that. You have your education and some practical experience; you may even be an expert in certain professional fields. But all of that will seem somewhat irrelevant and unrelated to the challenges you will face cross-culturally. You will have a few weeks of orientation and a period of language study, and then you will find yourself in a strange culture, in the midst of strange people and wonder, *What do we do now? How do we reach these people? This is not like our church in Georgia or Texas!*

You have been recognized as being spiritually mature, and you have learned the importance of spending time with God each day. But as you arrive on your field of service and are overwhelmed by the needs of a lost world, you will realize more than ever how essential is time with God each day as you seek Him for guidance and wisdom. The Lord impressed the writer of Proverbs of the importance of wisdom. He said it was more valuable than all the wealth in the world and was to be desired more than anything else; the Scripture also reveals that God was the source of that wisdom. In Proverbs 8:14, God says, "Counsel is mine and sound wisdom; I am understanding, power is mine" (NASB).

Note four things that God provides which you are going to need: (1) **Counsel** is divine guidance telling you what to do. (2) **Wisdom** is knowing how to do it. (3) **Understanding** is why you do it. (4) And **strength** is the power and ability to do it. These are all a part of the equipping you will need for the task. You are going to need all four; and in Proverbs 9:10 we are told, "The fear of the LORD is the beginning of wisdom, and the knowledge of the Holy One is understanding." They come from knowing God and living in a reverential awe and obedience to Him.

COUNSEL IN KNOWING WHAT TO DO

In the last few months, Bobbye and I have had the opportunity to travel overseas; everywhere we have gone we have found missionaries who had faced situations not knowing what to do. You will be told hundreds of time to be flexible and roll with the punches, but you will likely be confronted with a difficult adjustment or a seemingly impossible challenge. I don't want you to be disillusioned, but many missionaries who have served for any length of time would probably say they are not doing what they expected to be doing, based on their expectations before they arrived on the field.

Now that is not to say they have missed their calling or been diverted from God's will; to the contrary, they have been obedient to seek God's counsel and to follow His wisdom. You may be the exception and find yourself doing exactly what your job description defined. But the important thing is to be obedient and trust God for counsel and wisdom.

A few years ago some missionaries began to be frustrated in their efforts to reach illiterate tribal groups. With all of their education, study materials, and resources, they felt frustrated to try to communicate and reach people within a culture that had no concept of reading and writing. They couldn't read Bibles; you could not give them study materials and tracts simply made good fodder for starting fires. But we discovered that these people had a rich historical legacy that was being passed on from generation to generation. Entertainment and knowledge were prominent in knitting the people together culturally, even without books and schools, but it was done through their oral traditions of storytelling.

Missionaries began to imitate this form of communication to tell the people about God, His love for them, and their need for a Savior. Not only did people begin to respond, but they would pass the stories on to others, and the gospel spread naturally and spontaneously. In the primitive, remote Muslim country of Mali, only twenty-seven new believers had been baptized over three years of work there, but last year 252 baptisms were reported once "storying" began to be used widely. One of the hardest things about storying is getting a seminary-trained missionary with preaching skills and deep theological knowledge to understand how to tell a simple story!

God gives counsel to know what to do, wisdom to know how to do it, and understanding as to why you do it.

WISDOM AND UNDERSTANDING

During the recent Olympics, some missionaries were a part of the delegation of athletes from two Muslim countries restricted to a missionary witness. Because of the sensitivity of the situation, I cannot even name the country or persons involved, but these missionaries lived in the Olympic Village, assisting with coaching and training the athletes, and of course providing an incarnational Christian witness.

Neither of these missionaries had been assigned to sports evangelism. One was an agriculturist, and the other was appointed for media work in a nearby country, but they had experience in sports and the coaching skills needed in these Third-World countries. They had discovered a platform of relating to people who had no exposure to the gospel. God gave them wisdom to discern an opportunity, gave them counsel in building contacts and relationships, and understanding in why they should respond to that opportunity.

You will find it necessary to manage many responsibilities, some of which you didn't plan on doing. Just last month we visited with Mark and Susie Edworthy in Poland. They were appointed for Czechoslovakia but, unable to get a visa, found themselves in Poland instead. Mark is a church planter and is actively involved in starting new churches, but because of the need to train church leaders, he found himself teaching in the seminary in Warsaw. Being the senior missionary, he has also had to work with national leaders to plan and coordinate volunteer projects and, because of his leadership gifts and skills, has just become Foreign Mission Board administrator for the Baltic missions.

How do you juggle so many responsibilities in addition to family needs and adjust to the time that it takes to live in a foreign culture? It doesn't come from your own strength! You don't fulfill a role such as that from the perspective of your own insights but only as you seek counsel from the Lord to understand what to do, seek His wisdom in knowing how to do it, and understand why you do what you do.

Strength for the Task

We have just had a recognition service for eighty-eight emeritus missionaries. They have served in every kind of culture and mission situation overseas, some for as long as forty years. Each one of them would testify that they could not have done it in their own strength; but they learned very early in their career, as did Paul, that "I am able to do all things through [Christ] who strengthens me" (Phil. 4:13).

Jesus reminded His disciples, "I am the vine; you are the branches. The one who remains in Me and I in him produces much fruit, because you can do nothing without Me" (John 15:5). We can do nothing in ourselves. The ability to bear fruit in serving God, winning people to Christ, and bringing people into the kingdom comes only through abiding in Christ and appropriating His power.

Paul testified to this truth in Galatians 2:19–20: "I have been crucified with Christ; and I no longer live, but Christ lives in me. The life I now live in the flesh, I live by faith in the Son of God, who loved me and gave Himself for me."

God will not only give you counsel, wisdom, and understanding, but He will give you strength for the task. That doesn't come automatically, however, but only as you walk in the fear of the Lord, committed and obedient to His calling, and trusting Him for the power you need in your missionary task. So give priority to spending time with the Lord in prayer; maintain an intimate fellowship with Him, and He will guide you and the missionaries with whom you work. He will give you counsel in knowing what to do. He will give you wisdom in knowing how to do it. He will give you understanding as to why you must do what you do. It may not always make sense as you seek to relate cross-culturally and communicate in another language. But God will give you insight and understanding. He will not lead you to a task except as He provides the strength and power you need to do it.

You are going to the mission field in obedience to God's call. You have learned to seek Him and to walk with Him. You have gained valuable experience and training along the way and will receive more as you arrive to fulfill your assignment overseas. But the equipping you need for the task comes from God. As you seek Him diligently and faithfully each day, you can be assured that He will counsel you to know His will, give you wisdom and understanding to know how to do it and why, and provide the strength you need for the task.

9

On the Potter's Wheel

Jeremiah 18:1–6

It has been a blessing to hear how God has touched the lives of those being called to missionary service. Each one has been redeemed by the grace of God and touched with a unique sense of call to take the gospel of Jesus Christ to a lost world. The diversity of their background and experience is not exceeded by the difference in the call, which sends them to a wide variety of assignments that could be orchestrated only by God. Some are going to traditional fields where God is moving in phenomenal ways. An open opportunity for witness in those countries is linked with growing national churches in extending the gospel to the fringes of lostness.

In recent years, creative access strategies have opened doors of witness in previously closed countries, and many are being appointed to take the gospel to frontier assignments where it has never been proclaimed. These locations call for unique skills and professional credentials. Reaching a lost world today demands training and experience in areas one may not have anticipated when they went to seminary in preparation for missionary service. In fact, contemporary missions require a flexibility and continuing adjustments even after one arrives on the field.

What God has done and is continuing to do in your life is not unlike the lesson the prophet Jeremiah learned as God led him to the potter's house. The Scripture records his observations in Jeremiah 18:3–6: Jeremiah says, "I went down to the potter's house, and there he was, working away at the wheel. But the jar that he was making from the clay became flawed in the potter's hand, so he made it into another jar, as it seemed right for him to do. The word of the LORD came to me: 'House of Israel, can I not treat you as this potter [treats his clay]?'—[this is] the LORD's declaration. 'Just like clay in the potter's hand, so are you in My hand.'"

GOD CHOSE AND SHAPED YOUR LIFE FOR HIS PURPOSE

The analogy of what Jeremiah observed was an illustration of what God was doing with His people, Israel. He had chosen them and sought to form them for a special purpose of serving Him. They were to be a witness to the nations of His glory. A part of His forming them, like the potter formed that lump of clay, was delivering them from bondage in Egypt. It included guiding them and protecting them through their wilderness wanderings and then bringing them into the promised land. Instead of faithfully fulfilling God's purpose, they rebelled and worshipped pagan gods. They chose to indulge in self-gratifying pleasures instead of serving God and living for Him. God could have rejected them, cast them aside, and chosen another people to fulfill His mission, but instead He chose to take that same, misshapen lump of clay and make them again as a vessel useful for His service.

Like that lump of clay, at some point in your life God chose you and determined a plan and purpose for your life. He began to form you and mold you as a vessel to be used according to His will. Some of you had a salvation experience at an early age that brought you into a relationship with Jesus Christ. For others it was later in life when a caring friend, or maybe because of a personal crisis, helped you understand God's love, and someone led you to a decision of repentance and faith that would change the course of your life.

Being here in Jackson, Mississippi, brings to mind that time in my own life, for just a few blocks from here I received Jesus into my life. A little way down North State Street at Tiger Stadium, behind Bailey Junior High School, Billy Graham was preaching on a July night in 1952 when I came under the conviction of sin and truly understood for the first time why Jesus had died on the cross. It was to save a ten-year-old boy who had been attending church all his life and needed to be saved and reconciled with a holy God. I remember pulling on my father's arm, whispering that I had prayed the sinner's prayer led by Dr. Graham at the end of his message, and wanted to join others going to the altar. As I walked down that aisle and across the football field to affirm and publicly confess a decision that had just been made in my heart, I felt a wonderful sense of peace and joy. Even now I can distinctly remember thinking, *I wish everyone in the world could have such an opportunity to know Jesus.*

I have thought back through many impressions that could be interpreted as a call to missions, but I believe at that moment my life, as a lump of clay, my life was placed on the potter's wheel and God began to mold me for His purpose. Even before you and I were born, God determined His purpose for our lives, and that is why we are here tonight. As the psalmist says in Psalm 139, "You . . . created my inward parts; You knit me together in my mother's womb. . . . Your eyes saw me when I was formless; all [my] days were written in Your book and planned before a single one of them began. . . . You know when I sit down and when I stand up; You understand my thoughts from far away. You observe my travels and my rest; You are aware of all my ways. . . . You have encircled me; You have placed Your hand on me" (vv. 13, 16, 2–3, 5).

Jeremiah understood this when he heard God say, as recorded in the first chapter, "I chose you before I formed you in the womb; I set you apart before you were born. I appointed you a prophet to the nations" (Jer. 1:5). God knew you before you were born; He redeemed you and called you to carry His message of hope and salvation to the nations. But as that clay was placed on the potter's wheel, some of you resisted His guiding hand, just as I did through those rebellious teenage years. You have shared how you chose another path, some in rebellion, others simply due to indifference and lack of surrender to God's will.

God Used Life Experiences to Mold You into a Useful Vessel

He could have cast you aside and let you go your own way. He could have chosen someone else to go to Brazil, Zimbabwe, Bulgaria, or wherever you are being assigned. But, no; in His love and grace His Spirit continued to call. Through experiences, both positive and negative, He continued to shape the clay of your life into the vessel prepared for His use. For some it has been many years since that initial call to missions as a young person earnestly seeking to know God's will. For others it has been more recent. But God was not diverted by your own self-will or circumstances that seemed to obstruct your being molded into that vessel, fit for the Master's use. God has continued to use pastoral and vocational experience, participation in a volunteer mission trip, and other experiences to expose you to the needs of a lost world and an awareness that your life was being shaped for a special purpose on the mission field. So you are here tonight, being commissioned, because you came to the point of yielding your life into the Master's hands to be shaped and used as He intended.

Others here tonight should be where you are, on their way to the mission field, but they have allowed something in their life to become an obstruction to God's plan. They heard God's call, but because of an unwillingness to leave the security of a successful position and a comfortable lifestyle in America, God's hand is no longer molding them to be that vessel for missionary service. I am saddened that after almost every service such as this, an elderly person will come to me and say, "When I was young, I felt God's call to missions but never followed up on that call; I have tried to be faithful in serving the Lord and supporting missions, but I know I missed God's purpose for my life. I wish I could start over." Some are deterred by a spouse who doesn't share a commitment to missions or family needs that seem to take priority. But just as God was patient and persisted with many of you, He is giving others an opportunity tonight to take that crumbled clay of their life and allow God to remake it consistent with His purpose.

But now that vessel is beginning to take shape. Some of you had to be reformed more radically than others. You have come through many trials in arriving at the point of crucifying the self-life and saying, "God, whatever You want to make of my life, I yield it to You." You may have been surprised to find that He made a missionary, or through your training in computer technology, or experience in agriculture or medical practice, He was preparing you as a vessel to be used in places that need to know Jesus.

God Will Continue to Mold and Shape You

Just because you are being commissioned as a missionary, don't assume that the vessel is complete and the clay has been formed into a finished piece. One of the most important things you can realize as you are thrust into a cross-cultural role is that your life is still in the process of being formed. God is still making and equipping you for the task overseas. You will receive orientation and training, but that doesn't begin to circumscribe what God will do in continuing to mold your life to conform to His will and plans once you arrive on the field. You will quickly discover that the flaws are still there. Self-will will continue to resist the Master's plan.

That sacrifice you have laid on the altar will come to life and manifest its fleshly nature through disagreements with colleagues and tensions and misunderstandings with national coworkers. A flaw will arise in the clay and resist the Master's hand that is gently forming you into His image through adversity and suffering when you succumb to loneliness and self-pity. The usefulness for which He is preparing the vessel will diminish as you allow the allure of worldly concerns to create a bitter spirit because of inadequate support and an exorbitant cost of living.

You need to continue to yield in submission each day, just as you have in surrender to His call. Count it all joy when you are allowed to suffer and be deprived for the sake of the gospel, and you will find the rewards and fulfillment more than you can comprehend. There is no greater joy than to have the privilege of being that vessel, formed and chosen of God, to bring the Water of life to those who may be hearing the gospel for the first time. God isn't finished with you yet; in fact, He is just now beginning to mold you into that vessel as clay in the potter's hand.

10

Serving Where Christ Will Follow

John 12:26

The popular song, "Shine, Jesus, Shine" reflects the significance of what is happening in the lives of those responding to the challenge of Great Commission obedience. They have been touched by God's love and drawn out of the darkness of sin. By His blood, they have entered into the radiance of His presence. And now God is seeking to reflect the brightness of His glory through them. May those of you being appointed to missionary service tell the story—shine, Jesus, shine; fill the land with the Father's glory. May the Spirit blaze in your hearts until the gospel flows like a river and floods the nations with God's grace and glory!

You are being dispersed all over the world. It is amazing how each of you has felt a specific call to a nation or people group in a unique place in the world! It is intriguing how God has led in your life to acquire certain training and experience in order to fill a unique assignment—some in direct evangelism or theological education, but others in music, business management, medical ministry, as strategy coordinators, teachers, and in agricultural work. In God's providence He is fitting it all together that Christ might be exalted among the nations and His salvation declared to the ends of the earth!

In the twelfth chapter of John, Jesus is preparing His disciples for His death and resurrection and for the ministry to which He had called them. He talks of His life as a grain of wheat which must fall into the ground and die in order to produce the harvest. Then He applies that principle to His disciples and to us, His followers today. "The one who loves his life will lose it, and the one who hates his life in this world will keep it for eternal life" (John 12:25).

You are going to the mission field, not because you love your own life, but because you are willing to lose it for Jesus' sake. However, it is the next verse that highlights the challenge you need to heed as you prepare to go to a foreign land, learn a new language, and identify with another culture. Jesus says in John 12:26, "If anyone serves Me, he must follow Me. Where I am, there My servant also will be. If anyone serves Me, the Father will honor him."

YOUR CALL TO SERVE HIM IS A CALL TO FOLLOW HIM

Too many times we think of our call as a call to do something—a job, a ministry, or a special task. You should not think of your call as one to be a missionary or to go somewhere such as South Africa or the Philippines and be a witness. Certainly, you are going to places where God has led you, and you are to be a witness; that is all a part of submission to His lordship, to serve Him, to lift Him up and exalt Him. And that requires dying to self and to your own self-will and desires.

But your missionary call cannot simply be encapsulated in the process you have been through in fulfilling the requirements of the International Mission Board and now being commissioned. Fulfilling God's calling is not simply a matter of going through orientation and flying across the ocean. No, it is a call to a lifestyle of service and following Him each day. That means nurturing your walk with the Lord—giving priority to your time in prayer and God's Word. It means being sensitive to hear what the Father says to you each day.

Recently, one of our new missionaries stood where you stand in response to a call to an unreached people group in a restricted nation. We thought we had all the contingencies covered for him to get a work permit, but his platform for entry did not materialize. He and his family went to a nearby country temporarily for an interim assignment while traveling in and out of his target country. They continued to fill in short-term assignments, and in their first eighteen months on the field they lived in fifteen different places before their visa was finally granted. It wasn't a very convenient lifestyle for a family with three small children. But with their visa finally in hand and departing to assume their assignment where God had given them a passion to invest their lives, I heard them share an amazing testimony. They said, "We never knew where we would be from one month to another this last year and a half, but one thing God has taught us during this time is that He calls, not so much to a place, as to Himself."

Jesus said, if anyone serves Me, let Him follow Me. When you respond to the lordship of Christ, it doesn't matter where you are; you no longer hold on to your own plans and a comfortable lifestyle. A call to serve Jesus means to follow wherever He leads.

JESUS PROMISES TO BE WHEREVER HE SENDS YOU

Not only did Jesus say to follow Him; He then says, "Where I am you may be also" (John 14:3). God is calling you to go where He is—where He is at work. There may not be any evidence that He is there as you encounter Muslims in the Middle East and Central Asia devoted to their Islamic faith with fanatical passion. You may wonder

Where is Jesus? as you see tribes in West Africa making animistic sacrifices, or Chinese in Taiwan praying to Buddhist idols. But Jesus says to you as a servant committed to follow Him, you are called to be where He is. He will not lead you to some place where He Himself will not be there with you. He concluded the Great Commission by giving this assurance; as you go in obedience to His call, He will go with you even to the end of the age.

Do you remember when Jesus sent out the seventy in Luke 10? The Scripture says, "He sent them ahead of Him in pairs to every town and place where He Himself was about to go" (Luke 10:1). Why would God send you to a war-torn country like Cambodia or Bosnia? Why is He sending you to an unresponsive, restricted place like Yemen or a hardened, humanistic society like Austria? Why would He lead you to take your family and live in the isolated, hostile environment of Russia or Central Asia? Why has He called you to the Philippines, Guatemala, Brazil, and Mozambique? Whatever the reason, it is because He Himself is there, ready to work through your witness. And because you are going where He sends you, letting the light of His presence shine through you, He goes with you to reap a harvest of souls in a lost world.

The Father Will Honor Those Who Serve Him

Jesus not only said that to serve Him was to follow Him, and that He would be wherever He sends you to serve, but He closes that verse by saying, "If anyone serves Me, the Father will honor him" (John 12:26). Appointment to missionary service is a wonderful, memorable occasion which I trust you will never forget. You are being recognized with a well-deserved honor for your commitment to go as an international missionary. Southern Baptists are proud of their missionaries, but unfortunately, for many it is "out of sight, out of mind." Fellow missionaries told me when we arrived in Indonesia that during the first year everyone will write; they are so proud of you and excited that you are serving where you are. The second year the amount of mail will begin to diminish, but your family and close friends will continue to write and provide encouragement. But by the third year you will look forward to an occasional letter from your mother! I hope that is not the way it will be; I trust you will have a vast host of prayer partners and intercessors who will lift you up, be sensitive to your needs, and continue to minister to you and to your family. But don't look for honor and recognition from Southern Baptists or the International Mission Board. Don't expect it from the people among whom you go to plant your lives. They will be unappreciative, sometimes antagonistic, and at best indifferent to your ministry among them. Your honor will come from the Father. It may not be in this life, but it will come from the satisfaction of hearing Him say, "Well done, good and faithful slave!" (Matt. 25:21).

You have been called by God and are going to a specific place to fulfill a strategic assignment in His divine plan to reach the whole world with the gospel. Remember, your call is a call to serve and follow Jesus Christ. You go with assurance that He goes with you, and the Father will honor you as you serve Him.

There are others who should be going in obedience to God's call to share the gospel with a lost world. Many have never considered missionary service because they have a concept of some kind of strange and mystical call that they have never received. Those whom God chooses to use are really just ordinary people, but they are people who have been willing to lay their lives on the altar in surrender to the lordship of Jesus Christ. When they made a commitment to serve Jesus, most of them never comprehended that He would lead them to a foreign country. But when that call came, it really didn't matter because they had already, like a grain of wheat, died to self. Those appointed to missionary service are not going because of an affinity for foreign languages or because they look forward to living overseas in an exotic culture. No, they go because they came to the place of losing their life that they might gain it for all eternity, and with it they will bring the sheaves of grain before the throne of the Father, that He may be glorified and honor received from Him alone.

Never in Christian history have the fields been so ripe for harvest. Hundreds of missionary personnel are being requested for Russia, the Ukraine, and all across Eastern Europe and Central Asia. There is an unprecedented harvest in Africa and Latin America. That harvest is sweeping across Mozambique, Malawi, Zambia, and Ghana. The fields are white with harvest in Brazil, Guatemala, Mexico, and Honduras. Barriers to reaching people groups that have never heard of Jesus are falling, but who will go? As the missionary said, "Jesus calls us not so much to a place as to Himself." Why are you unwilling to be that channel of witness, that simple earthen vessel through which Jesus can manifest Himself to the peoples of the world? Is it because God has chosen not to call you to missions, or is it because you have never responded to the call to follow Jesus?

When you respond to that call—a call to His lordship, to serve Him, to follow Him—it really doesn't matter where the place of service is. But that place of service may be where the laborers are few and multitudes are dying, waiting for someone to say, "I'll go. I'll be the one. I'll surrender to His will. Wherever He leads I'll go."

11

Characteristics of the Call

Romans 1:1–6

The Global Research Department at the International Mission Board created an interesting map a few years ago portraying the relative lostness of our world. The nations and peoples of the world are portrayed in varying shades of gray. Those areas that are evangelized and where the church has been planted are almost stark white. But those areas where the gospel has not been proclaimed are black, and most of the world is shaded to reflect the extent to which people have been evangelized. If you stand back and squint your eyes while looking at that map, it appears that you are looking at the black heart of a target positioned over Central Asia. As if you are looking head-on at the fuselage of an airplane, black wings extend both directions across the Middle East and Northern Africa in one direction, and South Asia and China in the other direction; this is what is called the 10/40 Window, because it represents a swath of lostness between 10 and 40 degrees latitude north across the Eastern Hemisphere.

It is not politically correct to attribute darkness to those who do not believe as we do, but if Jesus is, indeed, the light of the world, then those without Him are people in darkness. Our mission task is to push back the darkness by proclaiming God's love, reconciliation, and hope through faith in Jesus Christ. But the challenge of illuminating the darkness is formidable. It represents more than one billion Muslims across North Africa, the Middle East, and Central Asia; it includes multitudes in former communist countries, long deprived of religious freedom, and as many as 1.7 billion—one-third of the world's population—who have simply never heard of Jesus. Yet that darkness is being pushed back in an accelerating harvest and opening doors. Barriers are crumbling, and we are seeing the words of Jesus being fulfilled as He previewed His mission in Matthew 4:16. Quoting Isaiah (9:2), He said, "The people walking in darkness have seen a great light; on those living in the land of darkness, a light has dawned."

The apostle Paul summarized his call in his testimony before King Agrippa in Acts 26:18 by declaring that God had called him as a witness to the Gentiles, or to the nations, for the purpose of opening "their eyes that they may turn from darkness to light and from the power of Satan to God." Regardless of your assignment and where you are going, the task is the same—that those who are blinded by sin, in bondage to spiritual darkness, might be turned from that darkness to the light of Jesus Christ. Their blinded eyes must be opened to the truth. Satan has them in bondage to sin, but as you push back the darkness through your witness, they can be set free.

That testimony was at the end of Paul's ministry as he looked back on his initial call when Jesus appeared to him on the road to Damascus and called him to the Gentiles. He had served in faithful obedience to that call and had personally seen the power of the gospel bring people out of darkness to the light and from the power of Satan to God. But it is interesting to review Paul's call from a different perspective as it was expressed in the opening verse of Romans: "Paul, a slave of Christ Jesus, called as an apostle

and singled out for God's good news." Paul identified himself as
(1) a bond servant of Jesus Christ, (2) one called to be an apostle, and
(3) one who was separated to the gospel of God.

YOU ARE CALLED TO BE A BOND SERVANT

You are being commissioned to go to the nations, not because
you thought being a missionary would be a neat thing to do. It is not
because you are intrigued by the possibility of an overseas, cross-
cultural ministry and are seeking adventure. There came a time in
your walk with the Lord that you became a "bond servant of Jesus
Christ." This word is not the Greek word *diakonos* which is normally
used for servant, but *doulos* which means one who is in subjection
to another. There were millions of slaves in the Roman Empire in
biblical days, and this expression clearly communicated that Paul
was not his own; he was totally possessed by another—Jesus Christ.
He no longer had any authority over his own life and destiny; he
had relinquished all personal rights and privileges in order to be
obedient to the One who had purchased his redemption by His
own blood on the cross. The trend in our society is independence,
autonomy, freedom to do one's own thing, freedom to do whatever
brings pleasure or fulfillment, freedom to pursue status and success.
But you have turned your back on such egocentric, self-serving
motives and brought your life in surrender to your Lord and Master
Jesus Christ. Like Paul, you realize you are not your own, but you
are bought with a price. As a bond servant of Jesus Christ, you have
crucified self-will; you recognize that you have no right to your own
life but live to do God's will. You have no other option but to do what
He tells you to do and to go where He tells you to go.

If He wants you to go China, Uzbekistan, or Benin in West
Africa, you have no choice but to obey. Just as Paul went to Cyprus,
Asia, and Bithynia declaring the gospel, you are going wherever

God leads. When the door closed, he was undeterred but responded to the Macedonian vision and swept across the European peninsula planting churches. He testified that he had been called to the regions beyond, even if it meant stoning, beatings, imprisonment, and suffering in the wilderness or on a storm-tossed sea. He had no other choice but to be obedient to His Master. Response to your call was not an option because you, too, are a bond servant simply doing the will of your Master.

You Are Called to an Apostolic Function

We have a strange concept of a call. Most would not expect God to speak in an audible voice, but apart from a burning bush or a mystical Damascus Road experience, we are reluctant to acknowledge a personal call from God. The concept of a call could well be translated "summoned." That is a different connotation; it makes me think of being summoned to the principal's offices as a student, or when my father summoned me—it was usually to assign me a chore or to give an account for disobedient behavior. I'll not elaborate on the latter, but the summons came from one in authority. Whether or not to respond was not optional!

Apostleship was a functional office that was a gift to the church. We traditionally think of the twelve disciples of Jesus as apostles. After the betrayal of Judas and his self-inflicted death, the group felt God's leadership to select a replacement following the crucifixion, resurrection, and ascension of Jesus. This account in the first chapter of Acts reveals two criteria for one to be selected as an apostle. They were to have been with Jesus, a companion and eyewitness of His ministry upon earth. Second, they were commissioned and the ones sent to proclaim the gospel of the kingdom. In fact, the word *apostle* means "one who is sent."

Paul wasn't included in that original group of apostles, but he had a legitimate claim to apostleship. He had seen Jesus and was commissioned and sent out by Him, just like the others; in fact, his being sent to the Gentiles—to the nations—was an apostleship that was distinct. Most scholars believe the office and role of apostle was only for the first century in laying the foundation for the church and launching the kingdom. But you have a calling that is just as real and similar in function. Jesus appeared to you—not visibly or audibly—but your call is as real to you as Paul's vision on the road to Damascus, and He has sent you to the nations.

You have heard that summons from God to disciple the nations and to be His witness to the uttermost ends of the earth. It is a calling for every born-again believer, but you have heard it personally as a call on your life. Some of you heard that call on a volunteer or short-term mission project when you saw the reality of a world in darkness. Others heard that call as a child or as a young person at camp struggling with the reality of God's will for your life. Several have heard God's call as a pastor trying to reconcile the stewardship of your ministry among so many churches here at home when millions have had no chance to hear the gospel. Whatever the nature of God's call and circumstances, you responded and are being sent out in affirmation of your apostolic role.

Recently on a unique, clandestine trip to Iran, our group was touring an ancient Armenian church in the city of Esfahan. The walls of the church were lined with marble plaques commemorating Christians of a former era, some of whom had been martyred for their faith. As we were walking across the courtyard, someone noticed a marker that was identified as the tomb of Mary Catherine Ironside, a missionary to Persia who died in 1921 at the age of thirty-one. There was a four-line verse that was difficult to read. The letters were worn, and it took a collective effort to decipher it, but this is what it said:

> She heard God's call come follow, that was all;
> Earth's joys grew dim, her soul went after Him.
> She arose and followed, that was all.
> Will you not follow when you hear His call?

YOU ARE BEING SEPARATED FOR THE GOSPEL

Finally, Paul indicated that he was "separated to the gospel of God." To be separated means to be separated from something to something else; it means to be marked off by bounds or limits. In being separated to the gospel, Paul meant that he was leaving everything else behind—his heritage, his personal goals and plans, the allure of worldly gain, any compromise of moral standards—in order to declare the gospel of Jesus Christ. This was driven by his sense of indebtedness to a lost world.

You have recognized that God has seen fit to save you, and because of that you are a debtor to those in darkness. You have been called to leave other pursuits and ambitions out of a responsibility to proclaim the gospel to those who are lost. You have been separated from pursuit of the American dream, from bondage to consumerism and material gain, from fulfillment of personal ambition to declare the gospel and push back the darkness.

All of this is for the purpose expressed in verse 5, "We have received grace and apostleship through Him to bring about the obedience of faith among all the nations, on behalf of His name" (Rom. 1:5). That expresses why you are called as an apostle, surrendered as a bond servant, and separated to the gospel, that all the nations might come to obedience to the faith for His namesake—for the name of Him alone who is worthy to receive power and honor and glory and praise, Jesus Christ.

But I don't want you to miss the next verse, which says, "including yourselves who are also Jesus Christ's by calling" (Rom. 1:6). Many others here tonight should be where you are. No one is exempt from the call of God who desires that the light would shine on the nations and peoples in darkness. As God has opened a window of opportunity in Russia and throughout Eastern Europe, do you not hear the summons to share the gospel? As the barriers crumble and people groups in darkness who have been deprived of the gospel become accessible, will you heed God's summons and be the one to push back the darkness among the Baluchi and Balswari in Central Asia, or Bashkortostan, or the cities of Jilin and Harbin in China? Are you willing to be separated for the sake of the gospel? Have you come to the point of surrender in becoming a bond servant of Jesus Christ for obedience to the faith among the nations?

12

Running the Race

Hebrews 12:1–2

One of the joys we have in being associated with the International Mission Board is watching the race. We have watched many missionary candidates enter the application process for missionary appointment. For some it is a long and arduous effort to accrue the necessary experience, conform to the criteria for health screening, and meet all the qualifications. Following appointment, there is a time of orientation and then language learning on the field.

We see personnel as they return to the States for furlough periodically. It is a time of debriefing, refreshing, encouragement in the task, and further equipping. Then, each year we recognize and honor those who are retiring after a lifetime of faithful service overseas. They are passing the baton in the relay to a younger generation who will continue to build on the foundation they have laid; because of their work, new missionaries can push the fringes of lostness back even farther.

You probably feel that you have already been struggling in a race and perceive being appointed as a missionary as reaching the finish line in your aspiration to reach the goal of appointment. It has been a challenging journey to get to this point; you have stayed focused on the goal and been approved. But, whether you are being commissioned in response to a recent commitment to missions or a long pilgrimage, the race is just beginning.

We are reminded of the race you are to run by the writer of Hebrews in the first two verses of chapter 12—"Therefore since we also have such a large cloud of witnesses surrounding us, let us lay aside every weight and the sin that so easily ensnares us, and run with endurance (or patience) the race that lies before us, keeping our eyes on Jesus, the source and perfecter of our faith, who for the joy that lay before Him endured a cross and despised the shame, and has sat down at the right hand of God's throne" (Heb. 12:1–2).

You are going to encounter many obstacles, trials, and challenges as you go to the field. We are going to try to prepare you as much as possible in a time of orientation, but you will experience the stress of language study and encounter the red tape of government bureaucracies. Some of you are going to places where you will be unwelcome, places that are so sensitive that the location of your assignment cannot be publicly identified. It's not unlikely you will be subjected to threats and harassment. Your family will experience strange illnesses that will threaten your tenure. There will be days you will succumb to loneliness and discouragement.

But I would echo the charge of the Scripture that tells us to run the race with patience, with the goal of endurance, so that one day you can say with Paul, "I have finished the race, I have kept the faith. In the future, there is reserved for me the crown of righteousness" (2 Tim. 4:7–8). How can you avoid stopping short? How can you be assured of enduring to the end in fulfilling your call and accomplishing the mission God has for you in China, Russia, the Ukraine, or South America?

First, It Is Necessary to Lay Aside Any Besetting Sin

You are aware that we have thoroughly scrutinized your background and character references. You have given your life to missionary service and in doing so have long ago renounced the allure of the world and lusts of the flesh. Unfortunately, even missionaries sometimes stumble and succumb to moral flaws, but that is unlikely. All of us are vulnerable, and Satan knows how to exploit our weaknesses and those things that can so easily sabotage our ministry and witness. For some it may be a tendency toward pride and self-sufficiency. For others it may be a lack of faith to trust the future and every circumstance to God's sovereign power. You may find a servant heart to be elusive and realize that interpersonal conflict seems to be a pattern in your relationships.

We are told to lay aside anything that would weigh us down, any besetting sin that would hinder us from running the race and enduring on the field to which God has called us. I would encourage you to set aside only a minimal amount of household goods and things to pack in your crates and then discard half of what you have selected. Don't be burdened down by possessions and material things. You will find an abundance of furnishings and possessions divert your attention and your affection from Christ and His calling. What if they get stolen? So efforts have to be made to guard them and make them secure. What if they are lost, destroyed by fire, or go down with the ship that sinks as it traverses the ocean? "Things" can become a weight that distracts you from the task and inhibits running the race to which God has called you.

When you find yourself defending your rights, your opinion, your work, let Christ remind you that He has called you to die to self, to crucify your life that Christ might live within you and empower you. Do you know how you can tell if you have a servant heart? By your attitude when others treat you like a servant, take advantage of you, and do not give the recognition and honor you think you deserve.

Many forfeit an effective ministry, and some come home, because they are unwilling to pay the price of purity and devotion to Christ, to put aside the besetting sin and become weighed down by things that should have been nailed to the cross long ago.

SECOND, YOU ARE TO BE ENCOURAGED BY THE CLOUD OF WITNESSES WHICH SURROUND YOU

That is an easy image to comprehend in this vast auditorium, surrounded by all these people witnessing your appointment. They are here to support you, to encourage you, to cheer you on as you go to the mission field. But that is not what is really meant in this passage. I have even preached sermons on the imagery of a stadium filled with those who have gone before cheering us on as we run the race.

But there are two kinds of witnesses—those who watch as spectators of an event or an activity or sport, in which someone else is engaged, are objective kinds of witnesses. But those who give testimony of what they have seen and experienced are another kind of witness. It is this second kind to which the writer of Hebrews is referring. In the preceding verses in chapter 11, we have what is known as the roll call of faith. It includes Abel, Noah, Abraham, Isaac, and Jacob. The list includes Moses, Samson, Samuel, David, Rahab, and others who believed God. They ran the race and witnessed God's faithfulness. They experienced temptations and trials but persevered. The motivation and encouragement that we need to endure the race, to overcome discouragement when we are tempted to throw in the towel, are through the example of those who bear testimony and witness of having endured.

Most of you know where you are going, but you can follow God by faith because Abraham is a witness of one who, by faith, left home and family not knowing where God was leading. Moses' life is testimony, as a witness to you of one who forsook the wealth and comforts of Egypt to suffer with God's people. He was an example so you can endure suffering as you identify with a lost and hurting world that needs to come to Christ in other cultures. When the world in which you go imposes persecution on believers, and may even touch you, you are surrounded by a vast cloud of witnesses who were mocked and scorned, imprisoned, stoned, slain with the sword and left destitute, but they endured in a testimony of faith and give witness to you. Not only these Bible heroes, but a great crowd of former missionaries have been there; they went through what you will experience and bear witness of the reward that comes from running the race.

Each week we are usually notified of the death of one or two of our many emeritus missionaries. In fact, this afternoon our board observed a time of memorial for those who have passed away in the last six months. Even in our sorrow it was a time of rejoicing and praising God for their faithfulness, for the lives that were touched through their witness and for their influence which continues to multiply through the believers they won and discipled. They surround you as you are commissioned tonight, bearing witness to you of what it means to remain faithful and endure to the end. They are encouraging you by their example, saying, "Persevere, hold on, run the race to completion; be faithful to the end."

THIRD, YOU ARE ADMONISHED TO KEEP YOUR EYES ON JESUS

You may put aside every encumbrance; you will remember and look to others who have gone before and surround you with their witness of encouragement. But the greatest motivation is the example of our Lord who endured the cross, despising the shame and humiliation for the joy that was before Him—the joy of a lost world being redeemed and restored to the kingdom. You will never make it if you are going for the purpose of making your mark in the world and seeking to build your reputation as an effective missionary. You will never survive the tortuous agony of learning another language, being humiliated and laughed at because of your foreign appearance and customs, except as you have endured the cross of a crucified life. You, like Jesus, must be willing to die to self for the joy of seeing unreached people groups brought into the kingdom. It was worth Jesus giving His all, and He finished the task, purchased our salvation, and secured our salvation because He endured.

Dr. Jasper McPhail was able to open Southern Baptist mission work in India in the early 1960s because of his impressive medical credentials. He was a cardiovascular surgeon in Memphis, Tennessee; because of his expertise, he was able to gain entry into the country after applications for Southern Baptist missionary visas had been denied for many years. Eventually medical work was opened in Bangalore, where Dr. Rebekah Naylor continues to serve.

People asked Dr. McPhail, "How can you give up your practice and all it means here? How can you sacrifice what you have attained to go as a missionary to India?" Dr. McPhail would reply, "I gave up my life to do God's will when I trusted Him as my Savior. To sacrifice means to give up that which is of value to you. That which is of greatest value to me is God's will for my life. How can I consider it a sacrifice to go to India for Christ when He considered it a privilege to go to Calvary for me?"

May you run with patience, with endurance, the race that is set before you, by laying aside any sin or hindrance to fulfilling God's calling. May you be encouraged by the vast host of missionaries who have gone before and bear witness of God's grace and faithfulness as you persevere through trials and hardships. But, primarily, may you keep your eyes on Jesus and His example. He knew the joy of the ultimate outcome of His suffering on the cross. Like Paul who determined to know nothing except Jesus Christ and Him crucified (1 Cor. 2:2), may you be compelled by the indwelling presence of the One who saved you and called you. It is for the joy of seeing those from every tribe and people and language and nation around the throne of God and praising His name.

13

Finding God in Every Situation

1 Kings 8:22–61

An important and basic factor in going as a missionary is a deep conviction that this is God's will; He has led you to plant your life cross-culturally in order to share Jesus with a lost world. He has called each one being appointed out of diverse backgrounds. Many are not novices to what you face as some are missionary kids who grew up on the mission field. Several have already served two years or more as Journeymen or with the International Service Corps, and many have participated in volunteer trips overseas.

You are preparing to leave family and friends and the supportive fellowship of your local church. You have expressed a willingness to turn your back on the comforts and security of your American environment to face uncertainty, isolation, and even danger in order to share God's love and the wonderful good news that Jesus saves.

After twenty-three years of service on the mission field, and more recently being a part of sending out thousands of new missionaries to the uttermost ends of the earth, I have gained a little insight into what you will face. There is much I would like to share to challenge and encourage you, but the one thing I want to emphasize is that you go to serve an awesome, mighty God who is sovereign over the nations. You have no higher priority than keeping your heart pure and walking with Him.

King Solomon reflected this in his beautiful expression of prayer at the dedication of the temple as recorded in 1 Kings 8:23: "He said, LORD God of Israel, there is no God like You in heaven above or on earth below, keeping the gracious covenant with Your servants who walk before You with their whole heart." Solomon was overwhelmed by God's majesty and power. In verse 27, he says, "But will God indeed live on earth? Even heaven, the highest heaven, cannot contain You, much less this temple I have built."

You will find yourself in the midst of godless people and societies where immorality is blatant, pagan worship and spiritual darkness pervasive. You will become discouraged and wonder why there is so little evidence of God's power. But God is there, and He will hear your supplication. Solomon's appeal is that God would hear the supplication of His servant and His people Israel when they pray. Notice the context of this appeal in the verses that follow. When does God hear and respond to His people's prayers?

Verse 31—When anyone sins against his neighbor.
Verse 33—When the people are defeated before an enemy.
Verse 35—When the heavens are shut up and there is no rain.
Verse 37—When there is famine in the land.
Verse 44—When you go out to battle against the enemy.

These are all situations you are going to face. Like Israel, you will find God available and responsive to your supplication. He is not restricted to an earthly temple, but He goes with you. You can come into His presence wherever you are being sent. He will hear your prayer and meet your need.

SEEK GOD'S FORGIVENESS WHEN YOU SIN

He says of the temple being dedicated, "Pray toward this place. May You hear in Your dwelling place in heaven. May You hear and forgive" (1 Kings 8:30). You are going to be aware of your own vulnerability as never before. You may sin in allowing a moral flaw to emerge and manifest itself in your life. The stress of cross-cultural adjustments and frustration in language study may precipitate a latent temper or expression of anger, even toward those you love. When you do not get the recognition or support you feel you deserve, or conflicts arise between missionary colleagues and national coworkers, a root of bitterness may lodge in your spirit, and relationships will become strained. Satan knows where we are vulnerable, but when you fail and succumb to sin, run to God. He will hear your supplication and forgive.

PRAY WHEN YOU ENGAGE IN SPIRITUAL BATTLES

You need to realize, like Israel, you are going out to battle. You go to plant your lives in Africa where people are in bondage to voodoo and superstition, or in Latin America where the ritualism of Catholicism has given Satan an open door to rampant spiritism. You will encounter ancestor worship in the Chinese world, idol worship of Buddhists and Hindus, and the secular humanism that has dominated Europe and the communist world. You are being sent to a battlefield. You are venturing into Satan's territory. First John 5:19 says, "We know that we are of God, and the whole world is under the sway of the evil one."

Whatever your assignment, you will be engaged in spiritual warfare. Ephesians 6:12 says, "For our battle is not against flesh and blood, but against the rulers, against the authorities, against the world powers of this darkness, against the spiritual forces of evil in the heavens." As you engage the battle, sometimes you are going to feel defeated. When a government bureaucracy withdraws your visa, or when you are forced to evacuate by an outbreak of war or natural disaster, as several of our families have done in Serbia, you will find it is easy to succumb to discouragement and hopelessness. When the opposition of antagonistic Muslim or communist leaders expose your platform, you will feel defeated. But never forget, God is on His throne; turn to Him in confidence and trust.

TURN TO GOD IN TIMES OF FAMINE AND LACK OF RESPONSE

Solomon told the people they were to pray when there was no rain and blessings seemed to be withheld. In 1970, when we went to Indonesia, the largest Muslim country in the world, I was so convinced of my call and the power of the gospel, I thought the pages of Acts would unfold once again upon my arrival. Even though it was a time of harvest, I found that many were indifferent to my testimony. As the months went by without significant response and the showers of blessing did not seem to come, I began to doubt the power of God. I felt betrayed. I had committed my life and brought my family to a foreign country, paid the price in sacrifice to live in a strange culture, and God wasn't keeping His end of the bargain. But as I fell on my face before the Lord, He heard my supplication. In times of dryness and spiritual famine when no response is evident, be faithful in turning your heart toward Him.

There was an occasion when we went through a very difficult time; it seemed circumstances and both friend and foe had conspired to defeat us in our ministry. A longtime prayer partner wrote us. It was just a note scrawled in big handwriting on a piece of paper that said, "Keep the view from the throne—all that is swirling about you is not reality. God is in control." We were hurting; the criticism and personal attacks were real. But we were reminded to look for God's perspective and be reminded that His hand was on us; He had not relinquished His throne! Solomon realized that this was what the temple was all about. It represented the presence of God in their midst, and when they sinned and failed, when they were defeated in battle, when there was famine and the showers of blessing were withheld, they were to remember to come to God in supplication and prayer and worship, and He would hear. God does not dwell in temples made with hands, but He dwells in your hearts. He goes with you whether to the remote provinces of China or hidden away in the Caucasus Mountains of Central Asia. He will be with you in Russia and Bosnia and the Ukraine, in Malawi, Tanzania, Bolivia, or Paraguay—wherever you go.

BE ASSURED GOD WILL BE WITH YOU AND BLESS YOU

This was Solomon's closing blessing. He says, "May the LORD be praised! He has given rest to His people Israel according to all He has said. Not one of all the good promises He made through His servant Moses has failed. May the LORD our God be with us as He was with our ancestors. May He not abandon us or leave us" (1 Kings 8:56–57).

Last week we recognized seventy emeritus missionaries retiring this year after a cumulative 1,882 years of service. It was thrilling to hear their testimonies. One could not imagine all they have been through—we barely were able to scratch the surface in their sharing—but everyone, in essence, testified that God had been with them. He did not leave them or forsake them; He was faithful to His promises. So will God be with you; He will never leave you or forsake you.

RECOGNIZE GOD'S BLESSINGS ARE FOR THE SAKE OF HIS MISSION

His remaining with you is not for your sake alone. In the following verses Solomon says why God has promised to hear their prayer and supplication—why He would be with them: "That all the peoples of the earth may know that the LORD is God. There is no other!" (1 Kings 8:60).

God's promise to hear and answer prayer, to forgive, to bless in times of dryness and lack of response, to be with you in the battle is not for the purpose of simply blessing you, His people. It is for the sake of reaching the nations that all the peoples of the earth may know Him. That is why you are being commissioned in obedience to the Great Commission. That's why God reached down and touched your life and saved you. That's why He called you to leave home and family, to turn your back on the security of an American lifestyle, to trust Him and follow Him; it is so that all the peoples of the earth may know that the Lord is God. Therefore, the next verse says, "Let your heart be completely devoted to the LORD our God to walk in His ordinances and to keep His commands, as it is today" (1 Kings 8:61).

Many of you are going to places we cannot identify, where the name of Jesus has never been heard. You are going as pioneers to the last frontier of global evangelization where the gospel is yet to be proclaimed. Others are going to the fields of harvest, joining other missionary colleagues where God's Spirit is moving in power to bring people to Jesus. Keep your heart loyal to the Lord, walk in His presence and follow His statutes and commandments. Remember, He is there. Just like Solomon's assurance to Israel regarding the temple, wherever you go, God is there. When you fail, and you will, you can go to Him. When you feel defeated and discouraged, He is waiting for your supplication. When there is no response and you go through a season of famine and dryness, run to the Lord and He will hear. He will not forsake you, because it is His desire "that all the peoples of the earth may know that the LORD is God" (1 Kings 8:60).

14

The Call of Jeremiah

Jeremiah 1:4–8

Although those of you being appointed in obedience to the Great Commission represent vast diversity in terms of background and the uniqueness of your call, it is fascinating to realize that God in His providence planned your life and brought you to this point of missionary appointment. As He said to the prophet Jeremiah, "I chose you before I formed you in the womb; I set you apart before you were born. I appointed you a prophet to the nations" (Jer. 1:5).

You are probably feeling like Jeremiah did in response to that revelation when he said in the next verse, "Oh no, Lord God! Look, I don't know how to speak since I am [only] a youth." Not all of you are exactly young, but in terms of cross-cultural missionary service, you are novices and may feel overwhelmed by the challenge of having to learn another language and communicate the gospel among those in a strange country. However, notice the assurance the Lord will give you, just as He did to Jeremiah. "You will go to everyone I send you."

You Are Going Because God Is Sending You

Each one of you has given testimony to the fact that God has called you as a missionary. For some that call came as a child in GAs or RAs. Others came to a point of submission to God's will as a young person growing in discipleship and commitment. You probably had no idea it would lead to places like China, Bosnia, Kazakhstan, Zambia, Moscow, or Chile. But that didn't matter; you had made Christ Lord, and wherever He led was fine. You were ready to follow.

Many of you were already on your way to a successful career or had envisioned service in a local church here in America as God's place for you. You may have heard missionaries sharing their passion and appeal for someone to "come over to Macedonia and help;" you went on a volunteer trip, or served two years in a short-term missionary assignment. You probably didn't anticipate what would happen once you were exposed to the overwhelming needs of a lost and hurting world and realized there was the potential in your life of doing something about it. But having said, "Yes, Lord, I'll go in response to Your call," you are being appointed in obedience to the Great Commission.

Regardless of the circumstances, the events and people God used to influence you, the Bible indicates that it was all intentional in God's plan and providence. It is amazing to realize that, like Jeremiah, before you were born God had a plan and purpose for you. He consecrated you and called you to the nations. Oh, you may have resisted that call, sought to hold on to your own plans and the comfort and security of an American lifestyle; you may have even run from the Lord in a time of spiritual detour in order to escape responsibility for what He wanted you to do. But He had His hand on you and has skillfully and divinely manipulated the events and influences of your life to call you to the nations at this particular time.

You Are to Speak What God Tells You

God also says, as He did to Jeremiah, "You will . . . speak whatever I tell you" (Jer. 1:7). Though many of you have already had overseas experience, and maybe even developed some fluency in the language you will speak, most of you are facing a challenging cross-cultural adjustment. You are here because you have said, "I'm in it for the long haul." And that means, in effect, a stupendous adjustment in identifying with the culture, learning the language, and understanding the worldview of your adopted people in order to communicate the gospel. If you have some anxiety and fear about the challenges you face, you should. It will require a tremendous level of discipline and commitment. But never forget that God is the one who called you and sends you. The International Mission Board is simply His instrument and channel of support and accountability.

The apostle Paul felt the same way. You may think of him as an effective orator, able to attract people to Christ through his eloquent preaching and persuasive wisdom, but that wasn't the case. In writing to the church at Corinth, he confessed, "I did not come with brilliance of speech or wisdom. . . . I was with you in weakness, in fear, and in much trembling. My speech and my proclamation were not with persuasive words of wisdom" (1 Cor. 2:1, 3–4). But he went on to explain that his message was "with a demonstration of the Spirit and power" (v. 4), because, "I determined to know nothing among you except Jesus Christ and Him crucified" (1 Cor. 2:2). He spoke, not out of his own wisdom, but only what God commanded him to speak—the gospel of Jesus Christ.

It is not your ability and skills, but the fact that you go with the indwelling presence of Jesus Christ. He will speak through you. He is the one who will give you wisdom in what to say and how to identify with those you go to reach. It is His message, and, indeed, He is the message you proclaim. That means it is essential you walk closely with Him, maintain fellowship through constant prayer and

Bible study, and your life will literally overflow with a compelling message of His love and grace.

You Are Not to Be Afraid—God Will Deliver You

Just because you are going in obedience to God's call doesn't mean you will be exempt from danger. Many are going to places that are hostile to a Christian witness and where missionaries are not allowed. So why are you being appointed to such countries? It is because Jesus said to go and make disciples of all nations. He didn't qualify that and say go only where you are welcome or where there is no risk involved. His desire is that He might be known and exalted among every tribe and people, every language and nation.

You have discovered creative ways to access these places and innovative strategies to share Christ, but you will likely encounter opposition. It may come from a restrictive government or the religious majority who see you as a threat. Recently, two traditional, historic mission fields, Nigeria and Indonesia, have seen stability evaporate and rioting escalate between Muslims and Christians. Missionary personnel have had to be evacuated in recent weeks from Bashkortostan.

You will be in places where there are health risks and rampant disease. Fairly regularly we get reports of traffic accidents, carjacking, and families subjected to armed robbery. God's Word says you are not to fear; He has promised to deliver you. Being in the center of God's will is no guarantee that nothing will happen, but your trust and your confidence are not in the International Mission Board, the U.S. Embassy or a big wall around your house. Your trust is in God, and He will protect you and care for you. He promises to go with you and deliver you.

Last year in one of our annual regional meetings, a group of strategy coordinators gave reports on breakthroughs in their area of assignment and testimonies of God moving in phenomenal ways.

They did not focus on personal trials and afflictions—even though one of them almost lost a son to a strange illness and for two years literally despaired of his being healed and surviving. But reported seven hundred professions of faith among the unreached people group to which they were assigned. Another had experienced a period of conflict with national leaders and efforts to cancel his visa. His wife and two children were injured in a terrorist bombing. But thousands of national church planters have been trained, and there is only one remaining unengaged people group among the dozens being targeted by him and his team. Another almost died of kidney failure and was in the States on extended medical leave, but when he returned to the field, the seven underground house churches he had a part in starting had grown to thirty among two unreached people groups.

In conclusion God says, "See, today I have set you over nations and kingdoms, to uproot and tear down, to destroy and demolish, to build and plant" (Jer. 1:10). You are going overseas to serve an almighty God, the Savior of the universe, who is sovereign over the nations. This is an International Mission Board appointment service, but it is God who has appointed you. If He is sovereign over the nations and He has appointed you, you go in His power and authority, which is over the nations. Do not go in arrogance and presumptuousness, for it will be with a servant spirit that you are empowered to conquer the kingdoms of Satan and the powers of darkness.

God is sending you to "pluck up" the roots of fear and superstition that hold the people in bondage. You are going to break down the strongholds of traditions and culture that have enslaved the people to sin and separation from the Father. In the power of the gospel, you will overthrow the false beliefs and deception that have kept people from the knowledge of the truth.

And finally, he says you are going to build up and to plant. God is sending you to extend and build up His kingdom and to plant the gospel in barren fields. You are to plant the seed that it may bear fruit in a vast harvest of souls. As you plant His church to be a nucleus of witness and ministry, the gospel will spread and multiply until all people and every community will have access to the good news of Jesus Christ.

In recent years we have begun to see a phenomenon develop which is being identified as church-planting movements. Once people receive the gospel and the Holy Spirit draws them into a fellowship of believers to form a church, these congregations begin to reproduce and multiply rapidly beyond the involvement of the missionary and church planter. Critics question the validity of churches started without a missionary to disciple the members and train the leaders over a period of time. It is thought that a church must reach a certain stage of maturity before they can witness in other communities and start other churches. Such skepticism ignores the life-changing power of the gospel and the compulsion to share that good news with others. If the initial group of believers are well taught and sound in their faith, then they will be sharing exactly what they received; and it will continue to be shared to the second and third generation and beyond.

Your calling is to plant the gospel in a way that the fruit will remain and the harvest will continue to multiply from the seed you plant. The power of the gospel will supplant pagan beliefs and false religious worldviews. As you are faithful to plant the gospel where God is calling you, the kingdom will expand to the glory of God.

We send you out in confidence that you are being sent by God. He has appointed you as a prophet to the nations. He will put His words in your mouth and speak through you. He will deliver you in the times of discouragement, trials, and hardship that you might be His instrument to break down strongholds, overthrow the kingdoms of darkness, and build up and plant the kingdom of God to the uttermost ends of the earth.

15

Essence of the Missionary Task

Acts 26:18

It is fascinating to hear the diversity of ways God has spoken into the lives of those going as missionaries. Through unique experiences and impressions, God made each one aware of the needs of a lost world and brought an awareness of the potential in each one's life to do something about it. Regardless of how one interprets the call of God, settling down and taking satisfaction in a comfortable American lifestyle is no longer an option. You cannot continue to pursue your own ambition and personal success once you have been confronted by the obligation of compelling obedience to God's mission.

Those being appointed to missionary service are going to unlikely places that cannot be identified specifically because missionaries are not welcome in countries like China and the Islamic republics of the Middle East and Central Asia. But they are joining others who have discovered creative channels of access in order to plant their lives in a Christian witness where Christ is being made known for the first time. Some are going to seize the open door God has brought about in fields where there is a growing harvest. Assignments in places such as Bosnia, Spain, Malawi, Chile, and Bolivia match your unique skills with strategic needs. You have a clear perception of what you will be doing and what you will encounter after a time of orientation, initial language learning and cross-cultural adjustment; however, you can expect that to change to a more realistic perspective after some time on the field.

When Paul met Christ on the Damascus Road, he had only a vague concept of what God was calling him to do. It was to be a witness to the Gentiles. It was God's timing for the gospel to break loose from a narrow Jewish context and spread cross-culturally among the nations. Paul was the one God chose to take that message of salvation to the non-Jewish peoples and other nations. It is interesting to note how his perspective changed and how he understood his call in retrospect as he came to the close of his ministry. After extensive missionary journeys to Asia and the surrounding provinces, planting churches across Europe, suffering beatings, imprisonment, and deprivation, he shared the essence of his calling in a testimony before King Agrippa.

He says that God had called him to the Gentiles "to open their eyes that they may turn from darkness to light and from the power of Satan to God, that they may receive forgiveness of sins and a share among those who are sanctified by faith in Me" (Acts 26:18–19).

You probably have not had a dramatic Damascus Road experience, but God has chosen you to be a witness to the nations. At a time when He is moving to penetrate China, Vietnam, and Indonesia with the gospel, to accelerate the harvest in Africa and Latin America, you are the one He has chosen to carry out His mission. But notice what Paul came to understand was the purpose and intent of his witness. It was to open their eyes, to turn the people from darkness to light and from the power of Satan to God. This remains the essence of your missionary task today.

OPEN THEIR EYES

Paul recognized that most of the world was blind to the truth of the gospel. When I first went to Indonesia, I naively assumed that people were just waiting for me to arrive. Although it was the largest Muslim nation in the world, we found a phenomenal opportunity to preach and witness openly. But I was disillusioned to find the people largely indifferent to my message and often antagonistic. I came to realize that expecting a Muslim to respond to the gospel was like asking a blind man to read a newspaper. Paul observed in 2 Corinthians 4:3–4, "If, in fact, our gospel is veiled, it is veiled to those who are perishing. Regarding them: the god of this age has blinded the minds of the unbelievers so they cannot see the light of the gospel."

So Paul realized the essence of his task was to open their eyes that they might be able to see and recognize the truth of the gospel. That will be the essence of your witness as well. How do you do that? It is not by logical arguments of human wisdom and eloquent persuasion but by lifting up Jesus Christ. Jesus said, "As for Me, if I am lifted up from the earth I will draw all [people] to Myself" (John 12:32). Paul acknowledged this and expressed it clearly; subsequent to recognizing the blindness of those without Christ, he declared, "For we are not proclaiming ourselves but Jesus Christ as Lord" (2 Cor. 4:5).

The peoples of the world have been blinded by false religions, perverted beliefs, and empty humanistic illusions. In their blindness there is no peace and assurance but meaningless ritual, superstition, and futile hopes. Your task is to proclaim the gospel in life and witness. Let them see in you a living Savior. Proclaim a God who loves and redeems by grace and then demonstrate God's kind of love in selflessly giving of yourself. Lift up Jesus who died for them in a bold positive witness, and believe that through the truth and power of the gospel God's Spirit will open those blinded eyes to the truth.

TURN THEM FROM DARKNESS TO LIGHT

Jesus described Himself as "the Light of the World." Jesus characterized the world as being in darkness because it was devoid of light. There can be no question regarding the spiritual darkness that pervades our world as you see Africans in bondage to their fetishes and charms. When you travel through the Middle East and North Africa and hear Muslims being called to prayer from hundreds of minarets in cities like Istanbul and Cairo and the idols representing millions of lifeless deities in India, you see a vast sea of darkness. Multitudes have been duped by atheistic communist ideology. Worldly materialism and immoral values are sweeping developing countries and the massive cities of Asia and Latin America. Spiritual darkness literally pervades the nations and peoples throughout the world. As a recent convert in Central Asia testified, "When you live in the darkness all your life, you don't even know the light exists."

But we need to realize that light always overcomes the darkness. Just as the sun rises in the morning and dispels the darkness of the night, and turning on a light switch dispels the darkness of a room, so the light of Jesus Christ dispels the spiritual darkness of a lost world. Darkness never extinguishes and overcomes light; there is only darkness where light does not exist. That is why you are being sent to the nations—to carry the light of the gospel to the uttermost ends of the earth; in illuminating the darkness, you provide an option for those whose lives are spiritually darkened by sin to come to the light.

How do you do that? Do you remember the familiar hymn we used to sing more often than we do in recent years? "We've a story to tell to the nations, that shall turn their hearts to the right, a story of truth and mercy, a story of peace and light, a story of peace and light." That's it! God has equipped us with a story—a story of His love, a story that Jesus died on the cross and rose again so that whosoever would believe on Him would not perish but have everlasting life.

You may be going overseas to be a strategy coordinator, a teacher, a business manager, or to do medical or development work; but the reason you are going is to tell a story that will turn darkness to light in the lives of people who hear and respond.

Because you go in obedience to God's call, we can sing the chorus of that hymn, "For the darkness shall turn to dawning, and the dawning to noonday bright, and Christ's great kingdom shall come on earth, the kingdom of love and light." We are seeing a dawning among unreached people groups that have been in darkness throughout history until now. We are seeing an accelerating harvest on fields where missionaries have served faithfully for years, and the dawning is turning to noonday bright.

Two weeks ago I met with national convention leaders from throughout the Caribbean and Middle America. All over these regions there were reports of unprecedented church growth. Baptists in Cuba will be reporting over a thousand new churches and mission points started in the last year. Some countries have seen the evangelical population reach 25 percent of the population. Earlier in the year Baptist leaders from the Ukraine, a country formerly in darkness, reported 150 new churches started and over five thousand new believers baptized. We are commissioning you to go to the peoples of the world and open their eyes and turn them from darkness to light.

Turn Them from the Power of Satan to God

I would not want you to miss the implications of Paul's third observation. He recognized in retrospect that God had called him to turn the nations from the power of Satan to God. You are venturing into Satan's territory, for where Christ is not known, where Jesus is not Lord, the countries, cultures, and peoples of the world are in darkness and under the dominion of the prince of the world. First John 5:19 says, "We are of God, and the whole world is under the sway of the evil one." Satan is not going to roll over and relinquish his kingdom without a fight; you are going to be engaged in spiritual warfare.

That warfare will not only be manifested in religious opposition, government restrictions, and pagan worldviews but in discouragement, conflict, and self-doubts. Illnesses and traffic accidents may distract you and inhibit your witness. You will not be exempt from natural disasters and economic challenges in which essential amenities are no longer available in the market. You are likely to encounter violence and warfare, which are rampant throughout the world. But the greatest attacks will come in your own heart as you encounter temptations, succumb to loneliness and self-pity, or allow a bitter and resentful spirit to take root.

Guard your heart with all diligence. Whether the spiritual warfare and power of Satan you encounter is within your own heart or in confronting a lost world with the gospel, the battle will be won on your knees. The victory comes in walking with the Lord, claiming the promises of God's Word, and boldly proclaiming Jesus Christ. You go to the mission field not in your own strength but in His power and strength.

We are told, "The Son of God was revealed for this purpose: to destroy the devil's work" (1 John 3:8). Christ has appeared; He has come, and in doing so He has destroyed the works of the devil. He has already provided the victory, and you are the incarnational vessel through which Christ will turn the world from the power of Satan to God. Just as Jesus sent out His disciples with power, He goes with you and has given you all authority over the evil one.

So this is why you are going in obedience to the Great Commission. Regardless of your destination and job assignment, you are going to a people, a city, a nation that is lost and desperately needs to know Jesus. You are to open their eyes, turn them from darkness to light and from the power of Satan to God. But notice

Paul's conclusion; the purpose of this is "that they may receive forgiveness of sins and a share among those who are sanctified by faith in Me" (Acts 26:18). It is wonderful to think that the people in Cairo and Istanbul, people groups in the Niger Republic and the Philippines, and the other places to which you are going will receive an inheritance in Christ; they can know there is forgiveness of sin because you go.

16

An Open Door That Cannot Be Shut

Revelation 3:8

God has called you to join Him on mission around the world at a time when He is at work in unprecedented ways. He is saying, as He did through the prophet Habakkuk, "Look at the nations and observe—be utterly astounded! For something is taking place in your days that you will not believe when you hear about it" (Hab. 1:5). I want to encourage you to go with that kind of confidence—that God is doing a work in our day that is beyond belief. It is significant that you are being sent out as we are just moving into the twenty-first century. Yet the significance is not a new century, or even a new millennium on the calendar, but the fact that God is doing something unprecedented to exalt His name among the nations.

Look at the places you are going. We cannot even identify publicly where half of you are going to serve because it is in restricted countries and among societies that do not welcome missionaries. But God has given creative ways for you to gain access and to plant your lives among people who need to hear about Jesus. As you build relationships and give of yourselves with a servant heart to meet needs, as well as providing a value-added service to their society, you will earn credibility to share your faith and explain the difference Christ makes in your life. You are not being sent simply because of your abilities, education, and skills but because God wants to reveal Himself to the nations and peoples of the world. He has promised to go with you through the indwelling presence of Jesus Christ. So, whatever your job description and place of assignment, your task and calling are to lift up Jesus in a bold, positive witness and make Him known.

In order to emphasize this, I want to focus your attention on the message of the Lord, through the angel, to the church at Philadelphia in Revelation 3:8: "I know your works. Because you have limited strength, have kept My word, and have not denied My name, look, I have placed before you an open door that no one is able to close."

GOD KNOWS WHAT YOU DO

First, He says, "I know your works." It is not a coincident that you are here. God knows your heart and where you have come from. Many of you were raised in a Christian home and have been nurtured in the faith since you received Christ as your Savior as a child. Most of you, like all of us, have deeds that you are not proud of and don't care to have revealed. But even that is a testimony of God's love and grace that He would say, "I've got a place for you. I can use you overseas." It may have been a little disconcerting for the International Mission Board (IMB) to scrutinize your background with such thoroughness in the appointment process. Yes, we know your deeds, too, but not like God knows them. And not only does He know them, but He ordained them. He set the course for your life and fed into it the experience, the education, the interests that have made you what you are and equipped you for the task before you.

GOD CALLS YOU TO AN OPEN OPPORTUNITY

Then God says, "I have placed before you an open door that no one is able to close." Isn't that assuring! God, who is sovereign over the universe, is saying: "I know where you are going. I know what you are going to encounter. Yes, I know that there is a wall of religious resistance in that Muslim country. I am aware of the barriers of government restriction to open witness and worship. But I am going before you to open the door, and no government legislation, persecution and harassment, or cultural traditions can shut it! When I have determined it is time for the gospel to penetrate those places that have been denied access for centuries or where the Spirit is aflame in an accelerating harvest, no one can stand in My way." Do you think God would call you to India, Southern Africa, the Middle East, or the former Soviet Union, only to be frustrated and defeated by the obstacles and barriers? People may not be immediately receptive, but be sure, in God's timing, He has set before you an open door.

No one imagined a few years ago the kind of response we would be seeing among many unreached people groups. We went with the perception they were resistant to the gospel, but we found in many places they were not resistant at all; they had just never had the opportunity to hear! Beginning back in the mid-eighties, we began appointing nonresidential missionaries to develop strategies for targeting people groups and countries where they could not live. Soon after I became president of the IMB, it occurred to me that few were being deployed as nonresidential missionaries. I posed this question to Dr. Lewis Myers, who was then leading our strategy for penetrating the Last Frontier. Dr. Myers explained that once we assigned someone to a restricted country or people group, inevitably the barriers seemed to crumble, and missionary personnel were able to gain access and live among the people. It seemed as if God was just waiting on us to be obedient to the Great Commission; once someone said, "I will go," He opened the door. You don't wait for the open door to be evident and then say, "I'll go." You first say, in obedience, "I'll go," and then you will find that God, in His divine providence, has opened the door.

CONTINGENCIES FOR AN OPEN DOOR

Notice three conditions for this promise and assurance of God's providence and power opening doors of witness as you go. Although God is working in the world, whether or not you encounter an open door is contingent on what you do.

First, you have a little power. Never forget that the gospel is the power of God unto salvation. He has equipped you with a life-changing experience of being born again by faith in Jesus Christ. The testimony of that experience and the message of a God who loves us, even as sinners, and died for us gives a power beyond anything you will encounter on the mission field. There is no religious truth, humanistic philosophy, or self-sufficient lifestyle that can offer the power found in the simple truth of the gospel. And God has placed that power, the power of the gospel, in your hand, in your mouth, in your life.

When my family arrived in Indonesia as missionaries, we did not find an immediate receptivity to our witness. The results were slow, and I was frustrated. I was not only disappointed that God did not do more through my efforts, but I succumbed to a great deal of self-doubt. I thought of the promise in Acts 1:8, "You will receive power when the Holy Spirit has come upon you, and you will be My witnesses." I had no question that I had received the Holy Spirit in my life, but I wondered, *Where is the evidence of His power?* I thought of the example of the early disciples, as we are told in Acts 4:33, "And with great power the apostles were giving testimony to the resurrection of the Lord Jesus." I thought, *That is why I am here; why doesn't God give me that kind of power?*

I realized this was His will for me, just as it was for the church at Ephesus. As expressed through Paul's prayer for them, "That He may grant you, according to the riches of His glory, to be strengthened with power through His Spirit in the inner man" (Eph. 3:16). Then I thought of this verse, Revelation 3:8, and would find myself praying, "Lord, just a little power. I'm not asking for a mighty outpouring of your Spirit. I'm not looking for signs and wonders and miraculous deeds; I just want to see evidence, as a result of my witness, of something that cannot be explained by my words and activity, but only by Your power." God blessed us and allowed us to see people come to faith in Christ. It did not make sense for these Muslim people to turn their back on their society and religious tradition to embrace the Christian faith, knowing they would be ostracized and even persecuted. Why did this happen? It was because we have been given a little power, the power of the gospel.

Second, you have kept His Word. The ability to find and walk through an open door in evangelizing a lost world is also due to keeping God's Word. Do you want to be assured of God's blessings and see His power at work in your life? Are you praying that you can be an effective witness and see many respond? The Scripture says, "We . . . can receive whatever we ask from Him because we keep His commands and do what is pleasing in His sight" (1 John 3:21–22). You are going as a missionary because of your desire to be obedient to God's call. Your effectiveness will be tied to your continuing obedience to God's Word.

Jesus told His disciples in John 15, "I am the vine; you are the branches. The one who remains in Me and I in him produces much fruit, because you can do nothing without Me" (John 15:5). Then He went on to say, "If you keep My commands, you will remain in My love. . . . My joy may be in you and your joy may be complete"

(John 15:10–11). The key to an effective and fruitful ministry, as well as one of joy and fulfillment, is abiding in Him. And that comes from keeping His Word and following His commandments. Obedience to His will should not come out of a sense of obligation, because it's expected, but because of one's love and devotion for Him.

Jesus points out a third reason why He can assure you of an open door of effective witness.

Third, you have not denied His name! You may think, *I would never deny Jesus.* But that is what Peter thought as well. In the pressure of an intimidating or threatening situation, we never know what we might do. If we were to analyze it, we probably deny His name quite frequently when we pass up an opportunity to present Him in witness to someone. Do we not deny the name of Christ, which we claim as our own, when we reflect un-Christlike behavior and allow a harsh, angry word to be expressed from our lips? It is not unlikely that you will find yourself in conflict with your missionary colleagues or national coworkers. Such conflict, openly expressed and inappropriately resolved, can be very destructive to your witness and testimony. Jesus said, "By this all people will know that you are My disciples, if you have love for one another" (John 13:35). Some have denied Jesus' name by yielding to temptation and moral failure. It is denial of the character and holiness to which He has called you. When you fail to trust Him fully; when doubt and discouragement cause you to lose faith in His promises, you are denying His name, that name in which all the promises of God are sure.

So remember, you go in the power that He has given you. Walk in obedience and according to His Word. Do not deny the name of Christ in your behavior and attitude—in the way you live as well as in word. And He will go before you to assure an open door that no one can shut. Walk through that open door in confidence of His presence and power. Seize the opportunity to declare the gospel and expect God to work in drawing people to Jesus.

17

Stewardship of a Ministry from God

Colossians 1:25–29

In God's stewardship and desire to disciple the nations, He has called you out of a diversity of backgrounds and experiences to go to different places. Because God's desire is to reach the whole world and extend His kingdom to the ends of the earth, He has called some of you to Latin America, some to Africa or Europe, and others to Asia. But one thing is common—that is the fact that it is God who calls. Your call to the mission field is in response and obedience to His leading, and that has brought you to the point of being commissioned and soon to be dispersed to the uttermost ends of the earth.

In each appointment service I cannot avoid thinking of the apostle Paul, who was something of a prototype and example for those called to a cross-cultural witness. He expresses his testimony and passion in many of his epistles, but I want to focus your attention on what he reflected concerning his missionary task in his letter to the Colossians. He says:

I have become its minister, according to God's
administration that was given to me for you, to make
God's message fully known, the mystery hidden for ages
and generations but now revealed to His saints. God
wanted to make known to those among the Gentiles
the glorious wealth of this mystery, which is Christ in
you, the hope of glory. We proclaim Him, warning
and teaching everyone with all wisdom, so that we may
present everyone mature in Christ. I labor for this,
striving with His strength that works powerfully in me.
(Col. 1:25–29)

THE PASSION OF YOUR MINISTRY

First, the passion of Paul's ministry was to present every man
complete in Jesus Christ. Our world is filled with a plethora of
religious beliefs and expressions because man is a spiritual being
and is searching for that which we know can be found only in Jesus
Christ. As you go to a lost world, you are not going to find any lack of
devotion to religion. You will find Africans in bondage to fetishes and
charms, worshipping rocks and trees in their animistic worldviews.
You will find ritualistic Catholicism in Latin America that has been
influenced by spiritism. Buddhists in Asia place offerings before
idols in hopes of advancing their journey toward enlightenment and
nirvana. Muslims say their prayers to Allah five times a day but have
no personal relationship with God.

Absent from all these is a mediator between sinful man and a holy,
righteous God; a Savior who took upon Himself the sins of the world
that we might be reconciled to God and complete in Him. Even the
secular humanism found in Western Europe—a residue of atheistic
communist influence in many parts of the world—reflects a religion
of self-sufficiency that offers only futility and disappointment. One is

complete only in knowing Jesus Christ through a personal salvation experience, and that was the passion of Paul's ministry.

One doesn't have to live overseas and be an adherent of other world religions to be lost and separated from God. The Bible tells us, "All have sinned and fall short of the glory of God" (Rom. 3:23). You can live right here in America, attend church faithfully, live a good moral life, and not be complete in Christ. Only when you come to repentance and faith in Jesus Christ, accept His death on the cross as paying the penalty of your sins, asking Jesus to come into your heart and life, can you be complete in Him. It is only in Him that you can have assurance of eternal life in heaven and have that life-changing experience that makes you complete.

It was Paul's passion to present every man complete in Christ. You are going to be overwhelmed by the masses of people you will encounter. It will be natural to fall back to an attitude of hoping you can reach some of them with the gospel. You may readily resort to an approach of doing what you can for whatever may result and hopefully reach a few. But I would challenge you to be driven by the passion for every person to hear, understand, and respond to the gospel that all might be complete in Him. By what criteria should anyone be written off and denied the privilege and opportunity of knowing Jesus Christ?

As you see the congested crowds in the marketplace, as you get stalled in the nightmare of chaotic traffic in overgrown cities, as you see the endless apartment blocks containing thousands of residents, remember that God loves all of them. Jesus died for each one of them, and God's power is sufficient to reach them and save them.

I have often said that God will hold us accountable for every person who dies and goes to hell without an opportunity to hear the gospel. Likewise, God will judge His people for failure to reap the harvest and bring people into His kingdom where there is an open opportunity to do so. Our world is lost in sin. Jesus came and died that they might be saved and complete in Him. But He has given to us the task of telling them. Let this be the passion of your ministry as it was Paul's—to present every person complete in Jesus Christ.

THE PURPOSE OF YOUR MINISTRY

Second, the purpose of Paul's ministry was to make Christ known and to proclaim the riches of God's grace in Jesus Christ. It is significant that Paul described this as a mystery which had been hidden from the past ages and generations. He did not mean that the gospel was mysterious and difficult to understand; the word *mystery* means "that which is hidden, unknown, and unrevealed." For generations, God's plan of redemption through Christ had not been known, and it was Paul's purpose to reveal this mystery, to unveil it and make the good news known that there was salvation in Jesus Christ.

Among most of the people of the world, the gospel is still a mystery. Some of you are going to countries of Central Asia where people are locked into generations of Islamic tradition, covered over with years of atheistic communist influence. Multitudes are living among unreached people groups and have not yet even heard the name of Jesus. The gospel is still a mystery to Buddhists striving for enlightenment through their own good works and devout Muslims who pray to a distant, impersonal, punitive god. Jesus died to save them. God's grace is available to all of them, but not until that mystery is revealed can they come to the knowledge that is needed to appropriate salvation through faith.

That's why Paul said, "We proclaim Him, warning and teaching everyone with all wisdom" (Col. 1:28). He recognized that this was the purpose for which God had called him as a minister; he was to fully proclaim the Word of God to all people. To him it was a stewardship. That mystery had been revealed to him, and he had a responsibility to proclaim it to others. He described it in Romans as being a debtor to both Jews and Greeks. He owed a debt to those who did not know the gospel. Because he knew the way of salvation, he had an obligation to give that knowledge to others.

Realize that this is the purpose for which Christ has called you. You are being appointed to fill a specific job description. It may be to serve as a strategy coordinator or a church planter. You may be going to provide logistical support or gain creative access to an unreached people group as a business consultant, a sports trainer, or a medical worker. You may be going to do development work or provide media resources, but that is all secondary to the purpose of proclaiming Jesus Christ and making known the mystery which throughout history has remained hidden from so many.

THE PRICE OF YOUR MINISTRY

Third, you need to realize, as did Paul, that there is a price of your ministry. He began this passage by saying, "I rejoice in my sufferings for you" (Col. 1:24). He identified with the sufferings and afflictions of Christ for their sake. In 2 Corinthians, he wrote of being imprisoned, beaten, stoned, and shipwrecked. You probably won't have to encounter these extreme experiences, but just because you are being obedient to God's call doesn't mean there won't be any trials and difficulties. It would be a mistake to assume God is going to provide a hedge of protection and guarantee a comfortable lifestyle in gratitude for your sacrifice and commitment.

To the contrary, you are venturing into Satan's territory. You are going to find yourself in hot, tropical climates with no electricity for fans and air-conditioning. You will find yourself harassed by those who do not welcome and appreciate your Christian witness. Some of you are going to places where you will be hated and threatened just because you're an American. You are not going to be exempt from accidents and illnesses that will bring discouragement.

We are reminded in 1 Peter 2:21, "For you were called to this, because Christ also suffered for you, leaving you an example, so that you should follow in His steps." Your candidate consultant probably did not discuss that aspect of your call with you. If you were asked how you interpreted the purpose of your call, you doubtless said something like reaching a lost world or to proclaim the gospel in a foreign culture. How many would respond to the call to missions if the appeal were couched in the context of a call to suffer. Just as this was the purpose for which Christ came into the world, it is an unavoidable part of the ministry to which God has called you. The suffering of Christ was not just the agony of the cross, but in denying the world and selfish gratification, Christ suffered daily, and so will you. It is the price of obedience and following Christ.

THE POWER OF YOUR MINISTRY

Finally, Paul noted the power of His ministry; it was "Christ in you, the hope of glory" (Col. 1:27). What gives you hope and assurance of eternal life is the fact that a living Savior has come to indwell your heart and life. But that is also the hope of God being glorified among the nations. Paul could endure suffering; he was motivated and driven by a passion for every man to be complete in Christ because he recognized that it was the power of God which worked mightily in him. Whatever challenge he faced, he confronted it not in his own strength but through Christ who lived within him. He labored diligently to share the gospel, but his striving in the ministry was always with the reality in mind: "I am able to do all things through [Christ] who strengthens me" (Phil. 4:13).

You are going to struggle in learning a new language and adjusting to a strange culture. Just survival itself in a foreign country is going to be a struggle. It will be a challenge to communicate the gospel, the mystery of God, in a way that can be understood and draw people to the Savior. It is not you, your ability, and your skills, but the power of God that works in you and through you.

So you are going with the purpose to reveal the mystery of the gospel and make Christ known. May you go with a passion to reach everyone that they might be complete in Jesus Christ. Recognize that obedience entails suffering, but that Christ is in you, and you go in the power of God and His all-sufficient grace.

18

Earthen Vessels

2 Corinthians 4:7–10

Fulfilling God's call may have taken a long time and a meandering process in which God has led you through many experiences. He knew what was needed to bring you to this place in your pilgrimage of obedience, and He also knew the timing in which you were to move from a stateside ministry to an overseas witness. For some it has been a whirlwind pace once you heard and responded to God's call, but that call has been confirmed, and you are now prepared to go assured of sound doctrinal convictions and appropriate experience and equipping.

YOU ARE A VESSEL BECAUSE OF GOD'S MERCY

It is important to relate your call to an awareness of what you face in the challenge of Great Commission obedience. The testimony of the apostle Paul in the fourth chapter of 2 Corinthians provides several valuable insights. He said, "Therefore, since we have this ministry, as we have received mercy, we do not give up" (2 Cor. 4:1).

Realize you have received a ministry, a calling, from God. For some it is to go to the Last Frontier where people have never heard of Jesus; you are to gain access through a platform of teaching or providing some other value-added benefit to the country and the people among whom you will serve. Others will use your assignment to join a harvest in church planting in Africa, Latin America, Europe, and Asia where the gospel is being freely proclaimed.

Realize you are here only by the mercy of God. You don't deserve to be going and representing Him; in fact, you don't deserve to be saved. But because of God's mercy He saved you, and because of His mercy and favor, He has called you and allowed you the privilege of serving Him—being the one to carry the gospel to a foreign country. Paul says this is why he does not lose heart and get discouraged. His ministry is not of him, otherwise his own weakness and frailty, his own inabilities, would cause him to lose heart.

You Are a Vessel to Serve Christ

Just as God gave Paul this ministry, it is a ministry that has been given to you. It is defined in verse 5: "For we are not proclaiming ourselves but Jesus Christ as Lord, and ourselves as your slaves because of Jesus." Your ministry and your task are very simply to preach Jesus Christ and to make Him known before a lost world. Therefore, you go as a bond servant, a slave of Jesus Christ, to do His will and bidding. It is not for your own fulfillment and gratification but for His sake. You do not have the freedom to pursue your own will, to carve out a comfort zone and say, "I'll not venture beyond what fits in my plan and desires." You are called to be a bond servant, a slave, obligated to do the will of your Master. You go to serve others and relate to them with a servant heart. That is what will bring credibility for your verbal witness of the gospel—people seeing the difference Christ makes in the life of one who belongs to Him!

Do you know how you can tell if you have a servant heart? It is by how you feel when people treat you like a servant! You are not really a servant if you feel resentment when people take advantage of you or fail to express appreciation and praise you for what you do. Jesus illustrated this in the parable of the unworthy servant. He concluded by saying, "When you have done all that you were commanded, you should say, 'We are good-for-nothing slaves; we've only done our duty'" (Luke 17:10). Your call to the work of a missionary is predicated on the fact God has chosen you to be a bond servant of Christ. This is so your life can be a vessel—a channel or instrument—to reflect and proclaim the light of His glory in a dark world. Nothing in you alone is worthy of notice.

I have often shared the testimony of a couple who endured a very difficult assignment. They explained how they responded when they realized the challenges of their location and the sacrifice and hardship it would entail. They said, "We had to reconcile ourselves to the fact God had not called us to success and personal fulfillment but to obedience." We are just the container through which God chooses to work. It is not about what we want to do, about what brings us fulfillment and gratification, or about our reputation and reward. It is only about glorifying Him through obedience.

In fact, Paul describes us as nothing more than an earthen vessel—an ugly, clay pot. We probably should not describe you as ugly, but why would God choose you to be a container for the treasure of His Spirit? It is amazing that our physical bodies would be indwelt by a living Savior—a carton containing the precious truth of the gospel. It is important to realize it is not about you; there is nothing to commend you to God other than your availability, the fact that you have brought your life in submission to God's will.

You Are a Vessel to Reflect the Power of God

Because Christ lives within you, He has chosen to demonstrate His power through you, to show "this extraordinary power may be from God and not from us" (2 Cor. 4:7). In the verses that follow, He tells us how this will be manifested: "We are pressured in every way but not crushed; we are perplexed but not in despair; we are persecuted but not abandoned; we are struck down but not destroyed. We always carry the death of Jesus in our body, so that the life of Jesus may also be revealed in our body."

This graphic portrayal and prediction of reality is not exactly an encouragement to follow through in your commitment to Christ. You will be afflicted, perplexed, persecuted, and struck down. It goes with the territory; it is inevitable as a servant of Christ in this fallen world. But you will not be crushed or in despair, nor will you be forsaken or destroyed. God has said, "I will never leave you or forsake you" (Heb. 13:5), but He never promised to put a hedge of protection around you and insulate you from trials and harm. To the contrary, He told His followers, "You will have suffering in this world. Be courageous! I have conquered the world" (John 16:33). Peter alerted the believers to whom he was writing to expect suffering: "Dear friends, when the fiery ordeal arises among you to test you, don't be surprised by it, as if something unusual were happening to you. Instead, as you share in the sufferings of the Messiah rejoice, so that you may also rejoice with great joy" (1 Pet. 4:12–13).

Sickness and affliction come from living in places where sanitary conditions are unknown; the FDA has never ventured into the food markets of the places you will be living. Risks and dangers are incumbent in a society where warring tribal and ethnic groups propagate their hatred in an endless cycle of vengeance. You will likely find yourself perplexed in trying to understand how to communicate in a new language and explain your faith in the context of a worldview that has no concept of God as you know Him.

You will be perplexed by the interminable bureaucratic demands and all that is required just to live in a foreign culture. While few of our missionaries have been personally touched by persecution, they have been threatened. We prayed for Heather Mercer and Dayna Curry until they were released from being imprisoned by the Taliban in Afghanistan. Martin and Gracia Burnham, with the New Tribes Mission, were captured and held by Muslim guerillas in the Philippines for more than a year, and Martin was later killed in a rescue effort by the military. You will grieve as you see national believers being mistreated and harassed for their faith in Jesus Christ. It goes with the task of being a servant of Christ and a vessel to reflect His glory in a lost world.

Why doesn't God protect us and make us immune to suffering? What kind of witness would that provide in impoverished Third World countries? You may live in a comfortable Western-style house in the suburbs with other expatriate Americans and shop at the international supermarket with a guaranteed income from abroad; with that American passport in hand, you can always go home when war or violence breaks out. But what kind of impression does that make among a population suffering, living in spiritual darkness, and lacking the affluence you enjoy? They will not be impressed with the message and testimony you share.

But when they see you suffering from dengue fever, or witness your distress over the illness of a child; when they see how you handle the grief upon receiving the news a parent or loved one far away has died, then they are able to see the reality of your faith. Affliction and persecution are opportunities to demonstrate the reality of a living Savior; the victorious testimony of your faith that shows you are not crushed, destroyed, or forsaken could be the most effective witness you will ever have.

A couple of years ago, Tom and Gloria Thurman retired after thirty-two years of service in Bangladesh. I had the privilege of attending their retirement service in their home church in South Mississippi and will never forget Tom's testimony. He said, "We have experienced many circumstances we would not have chosen these thirty-two years in Bangladesh—earthquakes, floods, cyclones, famines, droughts, and tidal waves that took hundreds of thousands of lives. We experienced three robberies, one stabbing, four broken bones, 291 nationwide strikes that paralyzed the country, and 186 flat tires. We struggled with a difficult language, electrical blackouts, Gloria contracting leprosy and sieges of hepatitis. But we have nothing but gratitude and praise that one day God tapped us on the shoulder and said, 'I have a place of service for you.' We came because of the lost millions of this land. We walked with Him, and our joy has been full."

Why is this the way it must be? Paul explained in verse 10, that if the life of Jesus is to be manifested in our body, then we must be constantly identifying with His death in dying to self and to anything that would call attention to ourselves. It is to bring glory to Him and to Him alone. So, in order to be useful, in order for the light to shine in the darkness, God has assembled you, a bunch of clay pots, to be a container that will carry the light of His glory to a world that is perishing. Let that treasure shine brightly in your life as you go.

19

Flee, Follow, and Fight

1 Timothy 6:11–12

I wish your appointment to missionary service could be the kind of experience that would assure you of unconditional success and victory in your ministry. It would be wonderful if our gathering to affirm your calling, praying for you, and placing certificates of appointment could signify an anointing and empowering of God's Spirit as you go to serve Him in places around the world. To the contrary, we can only assure you that you are entering into a continuing battle that will be constant. The struggles you encounter will not only be those of learning a new language, adapting to a new culture, and encountering religious resistance and government restrictions. You will fight discouragement that comes from personal trials and loneliness. You will struggle with temptations born of pride and desires for personal comforts. Your very faith will be beset by doubts, struggling to believe the truths of God's Word, and trust the faithfulness of His promises.

I have often found Paul's advice to young Timothy relevant to new missionaries preparing to leave for the field. Paul had nurtured

Timothy in the faith and mentored him as they traveled together proclaiming the gospel and planting churches. But now Timothy was on his own, entrusted with his own ministry. Paul knew the challenges he would face to his leadership and the personal struggles he would encounter. In the closing chapter of his first letter to Timothy, Paul summarizes his advice with three alliterated words—*flee*, *follow*, and *fight*. "Run from these things; but pursue righteousness, godliness, faith, love, endurance, and gentleness. Fight the good fight for the faith; take hold of eternal life, to which you were called and have made a good confession before many witnesses" (1 Tim. 6:11–12).

FLEE THE DESIRE FOR WEALTH AND MATERIAL COMFORTS

Our focal passage began with Paul saying, "Flee these things." To what was he referring? In the preceding verses he warned against the love of money, describing it as a snare which plunges men to ruin and destruction and causes them to wander from the faith. He urges contentment as a factor in godliness. Your immediate reaction may be to think that this is not relevant to you. After all, you have left prospects for a promising career in America or a comfortable lifestyle provided by a church-related ministry here to go as a missionary. You have been briefed on the level of IMB support, so it is evident that you are not going as a missionary for the love of money!

However, you need to realize that you don't have to have riches to be vulnerable to the love of money. In fact, a deprived lifestyle and all you have to do without can easily create resentment and bitterness; you can be entrapped by self-pity, feeling sorry for yourself because of all the sacrifices you have to make. I recall reading a newsletter from a new missionary who admitted to feeling guilty because she found herself fantasizing about Walmart and Diet Cokes. It is amazing how difficult it is to be content when you dwell on what once would have been considered nonessentials when they are not available.

I wish we could provide a higher level of support than we do. I would be the first to acknowledge you will not get paid what you are worth for the endless hours of tireless labor for the kingdom of God. But we do provide support that is adequate for you to fulfill God's call. You will be given a place to live, transportation, assurance that your medical needs will be met, and other benefits. Yet every year there are those who resign, saying they cannot live on the meager support provided by the IMB—support that is higher than that of any other agency. They somehow forget that the call to follow Christ is a call to sacrifice, and they are entrapped in a longing for what money can provide.

I just returned from a meeting with all our personnel serving in Central Asia. It was the first time they had all been together for fellowship and equipping since becoming a separate region five years earlier. These were pioneers who have gone to the last frontier of the Great Commission, proclaiming the gospel among Muslim people groups long deprived of religious freedom under the restrictive, atheistic policies of the former Soviet Union. Many of them live in small apartments where heat and water are unreliable. They are willing to embrace an austere lifestyle, lacking the basic amenities we take for granted, because their contentment is based on confidence in God. Their godly character and witness are not contingent on things and what they have because they flee materialistic attitudes and desires for what money can buy. One of them said, in describing the joy of being able to share Christ with people who have never heard, "I cannot believe I get paid for doing what I get to do!"

FOLLOW CHARACTERISTICS THAT PRESENT A GOOD WITNESS

Fleeing the love of money and carnal values of the world, Paul then tells Timothy to follow after righteousness, godliness, faith, love, perseverance, and gentleness. He was to deliberately and intentionally pursue the things that would give a good confession in the presence of many witnesses.

You see, people are going to be observing your life because you are different. You are a foreigner, an outsider, who has come to live among them. You can't just blend in and get lost in the crowd. They will see you as an American and, hopefully, as a Christian; you are someone who is distinct relative to their nationality and religion. What will they see? What will they think of you and your witness? The impressions that are formed will not be determined by your role, your humanitarian projects and programs, but by the life you live and the relationships with those around you. This is why we say you are being sent to an incarnational witness; it is so people may see in your character and the way you live the reality of your faith.

Several years ago a pioneer missionary who was the first to be assigned to a closed Muslim country moved with his family into a local community. They adopted local dress and customs as much as possible. This meant the wife seldom could go outside, and when she did, she had to be covered head to toe with a burka. The husband participated in community events and work projects. He became known for helping people with special needs and assisting in humanitarian projects. He was invited to sit on the village council of elders. One day a visiting dignitary came and asked why this foreigner was there. The local elders explained, "Yes, he is a foreigner, but he is one of us; he is an American, but he is a good man." The way he lived built relationships, earned credibility, and opened doors for witness.

You must constantly be conscious of striving to live a righteous life characterized by godliness, faith, love, perseverance, and gentleness. This list is almost parallel to the fruit of the Spirit listed in the fifth chapter of Galatians. The reality is that you cannot be this kind of person except by the Holy Spirit within you. People will hear your preaching and the words of your witness, but what you say will be meaningless unless they see the reality of Jesus in your life through godly character. Will they see a victorious faith that perseveres when you experience a debilitating illness, suffer the loss of a loved one far away in America, or don't have the gratification of seeing fruit from your labors? Will they see a selfless, sacrificial love exhibited when people abuse you, defraud you, ridicule you, threaten you, or take advantage of you? Will they see a gentleness of spirit that is a radical contrast to the self-serving, vindictive attitudes common to their society? Many witnesses will be observing your life. If you follow these things, it will validate your confession and result in many laying hold of eternal life.

FIGHT THE GOOD FIGHT OF FAITH

The admonition to fight may seem incongruent with your role as a missionary, for you are going to love, befriend, and influence people to come to Christ. But Paul was aware that Timothy was being sent into enemy territory to engage in spiritual warfare—just as you are. Satan, the god of this world, will not easily relinquish his dominion over the hearts and lives of those in spiritual bondage to the powers of darkness and deception. If the kingdoms of this world are to become the kingdoms of our Lord, you must fight a fight of faith. When Paul was facing the inevitable end of his life and ministry, he testified, "I have fought the good fight, I have finished the race, I have kept the faith" (2 Tim. 4:7).

We are told in 1 John 5:4, "This is the victory that has overcome the world—even our faith." First Peter 5:8–9 warns us, "Your adversary the Devil is prowling like a roaring lion, looking for anyone he can devour. Resist him, firm in the faith." That victory is not just your faith that brought you salvation in Jesus Christ, but it is the faith to believe God, to believe the truth and promises of His Word when all evidence is to the contrary. You may quickly succumb to the perception that your people group is resistant to the gospel, you cannot expect a response, and the opposition to church planting is too great. But the Scripture tells us that "the earth will be filled with the knowledge of the LORD's glory, as the waters cover the sea" (Hab. 2:14). We have the assurance that one day there will be those from every tribe, people, tongue, and nation represented around the throne of God. Believe it, claim it, hold firm in your faith, and the victory will be yours.

You do not fight this warfare with the weapons of this world but with weapons that are "powerful through God for the demolition of strongholds. We demolish arguments and every high-minded thing that is raised up against the knowledge of God, taking every thought captive to the obedience of Christ" (2 Cor. 10:4–5). Mark Stevens is the strategy coordinator for Muslim tribal groups on the island of Mindanao in the Philippines. Last year he reported on the church-planting movements taking place and the fact there remains only one group yet to be engaged with the gospel. It was a testimony of successful harvest, but it was preceded by discouragement and conflict when national leaders tried to get him kicked out of the country, his wife and children were injured in a terrorist bombing, and churches were unresponsive to his vision and training. There were many challenges, conflicts, and trials when he could have easily thrown in the towel, considered the effort futile, and gone home. But he never lost hope; he held to the vision and fought the fight of faith and prevailed.

So as you go, flee the temptation to hold on to comforts and the materialistic values of this world. Follow after those characteristics that will empower your witness and validate your testimony, and fight the good fight of faith, holding on to the vision of that day when every knee shall bow and every tongue confess that Jesus is Lord to the glory of God the Father.

20

Serving Without Shame

Philippians 1:1–21

Philippians is one of my favorite books of the Bible. I find that verses from this epistle of Paul frequently infringe upon my devotional thoughts and are spontaneously injected into my conversation and messages. I have used a number of the more prominent themes and passages from this book in appointment messages in the past.

I have encouraged humility and a servant heart by challenging missionaries to have the mind of Christ, who emptied Himself and took the form of a bond servant. I have challenged new appointees to emulate Paul and press toward the mark of the high calling of God. I have charged them to have his passion to know Christ, the power of His resurrection, and the fellowship of His sufferings. They have been reminded that we can do all things through Christ who strengthens us and have been admonished to be content in all things, to be anxious in nothing, but to submit their requests to God with thanksgiving and assurance His peace will guard their hearts and minds. I have often concluded a message with the vision of Philippians 2:10–11, when one day every knee will bow and every tongue confess that Jesus is Lord to the glory of God the Father.

In once again reading through Philippians, I was impressed to highlight some valuable points from chapter 1. First of all, the book begins by identifying those sending this epistle as Paul and Timothy who called themselves bond servants of Christ Jesus. That's what you are—bond servants of Jesus Christ. You have turned away from personal ambition. Some of you have left prominent ministries or successful careers, not just to go do missionary work but to be a bond servant of Jesus Christ. What you are is far more important than what you do. You will be frustrated, and actually worthless, if you think you are going to the mission field to accomplish anything for God in your own ability. You are being appointed a missionary because you have said, "Not my will, but Thine." You are here, regardless of your assignment and role, because of a desire to serve Christ and be obedient wherever He leads and in whatever task He places before you. Obedience is not an option because you are a bond servant of Christ.

Also, in the way of introduction, another parallel to Paul and Timothy is your relationship to those gathered supporting you and celebrating your appointment to missionary service. They are a large group of family and friends and those from your church that have had a part in nurturing your spiritual growth and will be a vicarious part of what you do to carry the gospel around the world. Paul says, "I give thanks to my God for every remembrance of you" (Phil. 1:3). You have to be thankful as you recall what so many have invested in your life. As you remember a devoted mother, a Sunday school teacher or friend who led you to profess Jesus as your Savior, you have to be grateful. You are thankful for those who discipled you in your walk with the Lord, encouraged you in Bible study and prayer; for campus ministers who provided opportunities for ministry and missions involvement, for seminary professors who unfolded the deeper truths of God's Word and equipped you for the calling you are prepared to fulfill. As you are separated from them in your overseas assignment, you will grow in your thankfulness for every remembrance and the fact that they will be praying for you with joy. They will be participants in the gospel as you fulfill your calling.

I suggest that the theme of what Paul goes on to share in this first chapter of Philippians is "Serving Without Shame." This grows primarily out of his personal experience but also from his understanding of an intimate relationship with God. How can you fulfill your calling faithfully and unashamed, regardless of the results and what you will encounter?

GOD WILL PERFECT THE WORK THAT HE IS BEGINNING TO DO IN YOU

First, be confident that God will continue to work in your life to grow you, develop and mature you, and perfect all that He wants you to be in Christ. Verse 6 says, "I am sure of this, that He who started a good work in you will carry it on to completion until the day of Christ Jesus." You have done a lot to qualify for missionary appointment. You have completed education requirements and exemplified competence in ministry and professional skills. You have reflected a level of spiritual maturity and giftedness for your assignment. But God is not finished with you yet. In fact, I would say He has not even gotten started!

The mission field is going to put you through the refiner's fire. You will experience the initial stress of cross-cultural adjustments, the challenge of learning a new language, and the sacrifice of living without amenities and comforts that you have taken for granted here. Whether or not you have the spiritual resources for coping will be revealed. When you don't see immediate results and fruit from your witness and ministry, you will discover that there is a need for God to continue to grow your faith beyond where it is now.

Earlier this month, our staff was blessed in our annual staff retreat to have Dr. Mac Brunson as our speaker. He chose as his topic, "Growing Through What You Are Going Through." His messages focused on growing through waiting, growing through failure, growing through dealing with difficult people, and growing through discouragement—relevant situations we all constantly experience. Always realize that God is on His throne, and He allows us to encounter these situations because He wants to use them to grow us, to strengthen us, and to teach us the lessons that are essential if we are going to serve Him effectively.

Understand that God is not primarily concerned about your health, comfort, safety, and welfare. He does promise to bless us, protect us, and care for us, but His primary concern is to be glorified in our lives and to be glorified among the nations. Sometimes suffering and trials are the greatest opportunity we have to reflect God's glory. Often it is through suffering that the gospel is planted among unreached people groups, so that God can be exalted and glorified. God has saved you, redeemed you, and called you. He is at work in your life so that He might perfect you and your ministry, and He will continue to work until the day of Jesus Christ when He takes you home. We are told God's purpose is that you may "determine what really matters and can be pure and blameless . . . filled with the fruit of righteousness . . . to the glory and praise of God" (Phil. 1:10–11).

GOD WILL USE YOUR CIRCUMSTANCES FOR THE PROGRESS OF THE GOSPEL

Another point highlighted by Paul is the fact that God will use your circumstances for the progress of the gospel. This is one of

Paul's prison epistles. Having been arrested in Jerusalem, he had languished in prison in Caesarea, his case unresolved by a sequence of Roman governors. Finally, he had appealed to Caesar rather than being released to the conspiring injustice of the Jewish authorities. En route he suffered shipwreck and survived the fatal bite of a venomous snake. He had endured earlier imprisonments, beatings, stoning, and persecution. We don't know how long he continued in chains until his eventual martyrdom, but he reflected upon those experiences in Philippians 1:12–14:

> Now I want you to know, brothers, that what
> has happened to me has actually resulted in the
> advancement of the gospel, so that it has become known
> throughout the whole imperial guard, and to everyone
> else, that my imprisonment is for Christ. Most of the
> brothers in the Lord have gained confidence from my
> imprisonment and dare even more to speak the message
> fearlessly.

At this point, you all have visions of what you are going to do when you arrive on the mission field. You have a definite sense of God's call to the specific field and assignment that fits your gifts and experience. Many of you are going to what we call "the Last Frontier" where people have never heard the gospel; you have dreams of planting the gospel among an unreached people group. Others are going to established fields and envision joining the growing harvest of church growth. You are confident of being able to share the gospel with the lost, disciple believers, and plant churches. But it is not unlikely that, instead of those dreams and aspirations, you will find yourself in prison. Maybe not in a literal prison, though occasionally we have had missionaries arrested and detained. But you will find yourself in a prison of bondage to government legal restrictions that limit what you can do. You may find yourself in a prison of debilitating illnesses that inhibit your ability to fulfill your assignment. Intimidation by Muslim cultures, warfare and terrorist threats, or even interpersonal conflict with your colleagues or national coworkers may seem like a prison, restricting your creative and innovative initiatives that you feel are the key to extending the kingdom of God.

How do you deal with your circumstances when plans are diverted and situations beyond your control bring obstacles to your work? Paul was undeterred by his imprisonment. He simply used it to share the gospel with his Praetorian guard, those who would probably have never heard if Paul had been free to carry out his own plans. When the believers saw his boldness, even as a prisoner, it gave them greater courage to witness and to speak the Word of God without fear. Isn't that what you want to see result from your life and ministry—everyone to hear and know the gospel? Don't you want believers who you go to work among being encouraged with a boldness to share their faith because of the example they have seen in your life?

The question is not whether you will encounter trials, disappointments, and personal setbacks or not. The issue is how you will respond. Will you allow them to strengthen your faith and build your confidence in God's power and sovereignty? Recognize that your circumstances are an opportunity for the progress of the gospel.

GOD IS SEEKING TO BE EXALTED IN YOUR LIFE

Finally, realize that God is seeking to be exalted in your life. Your being sent out is really not about your assignment or the location where you may serve. It is not about your obedience to God's call to go as a missionary. It doesn't really matter where you go or what your assignment is, but it is all about exalting Christ in the life that you live. You are being sent to be an incarnational witness; the most effective witness you will have is to live out the reality of Christ in your life before a lost world. You could continue to be an effective witness right here at home and, in fact, maybe win more people to the Lord than where you are going. But how will a lost world know Jesus unless someone is willing to plant their lives among them and let them see the reality of a living Savior.

You are going to a world where people are suffering and hopeless. They live in the midst of conflict and despair. They are not impressed by your affluent Western lifestyle. But when they see how you react to suffering an injustice, when they see you identifying with their hurts and sorrows, it is an opportunity for them to see Christ and His love in you. Paul wasn't ashamed of his arrest. There was no shame or vindictive spirit because he had been mistreated, his own plans curtailed, and his very life threatened. This is how he explained it:

> My eager expectation and hope is that I will not be
> ashamed about anything, but that now as always, with
> all boldness, Christ will be highly honored in my body,
> whether by life or by death. For me, living is Christ and
> dying is gain. (Phil. 1:20–21)

We are not sending you out to die in a hostile and dangerous world. Some have paid the ultimate price for their witness, but if you will die to self and are willing to die that Christ might be exalted among the nations, then your life will be one that exalts and glorifies Christ. You can say with Paul, in whatever you encounter, I am not ashamed, for Christ has been exalted.

So, recognize that God will continue to work in you on the mission field to shape and perfect what He has begun in bringing you to this point of obedience. Realize whatever circumstances you experience, that God can use them for the progress of the gospel. And remember, His greatest desire is to be glorified and exalted in your life!

21

Are We Blind Also?

John 9:39–41

T he apostle Paul expressed the essence of our missionary task in his testimony before King Agrippa in Acts 26:18. He said he had been appointed as a minister and witness to the Gentiles, "to open their eyes so that they may turn from darkness to light and from the power of Satan to God." Your witness among the nations is not just simply a matter of proclaiming the gospel; missions and evangelism are opening eyes that are blinded to the truth of God by traditions, culture, and perverted religious worldviews. It is engaging in spiritual warfare in order to bring souls out of darkness to the light of the gospel and deliver them from the power of Satan to God.

Paul said in Colossians 1:6 that all over the world the gospel was multiplying and bearing fruit. Romans 1:16 reminds us that the gospel is the power of God unto salvation for all who believe. As the gospel is proclaimed, Jesus is actively opening the eyes and understanding of those who are spiritually blind and giving them a new life. But in the Gospels, He demonstrated His power to literally give sight to those who are physically blind. There are three accounts of such miracles, the most extensive of which is found in the ninth chapter of John. This entire chapter is devoted to the account of Jesus healing the man who was blind from birth.

This was a remarkable demonstration of the power and mercy of God, but it stirred quite a controversy in the temple that day. The Pharisees denied the fact that such a miracle could have occurred since Jesus was obviously a sinner and violated their laws of the Sabbath. They argued about whether or not this was the same man who had been blind. The disciples didn't do much better. Instead of acknowledging the miracle and praising God, they became embroiled in a theological argument about whether the man had been born blind because of his own sin or the sin of his parents. As the controversy continued, the Pharisees and religious leaders began to sense that what Jesus was saying had something to do with them more than the blind man. This is reflected in the dialogue at the conclusion of the chapter.

> Jesus said, "I came into this world for judgment, in order that those who do not see will see and those who do see will become blind." Some of the Pharisees who were with Him heard these things and asked Him, "We aren't blind too, are we?" "If you were blind," Jesus told them, "you wouldn't have sin. But now that you say, 'We see'—your sin remains." (John 9:39–41)

The Pharisees did not realize that they were the ones who were blind. They had all their theological systems wrapped up in a neat little package, but they were actually blind to spiritual realities. The man who had been physically blind was able to see that Jesus was from God; he acknowledged Him as Lord and worshipped Him. But the Pharisees were blind to this reality. They were so blind that they could not even recognize and accept a divine miracle, and because of their blindness, Jesus said they remained in sin.

The sin of many, today, may be in thinking that they see when, in reality, they are blind to the truths of God. Our postmodern culture has deluded many into seeing the world through self-serving, humanistic values while denying the truth of God. Even those, like the Pharisees and religious leaders, who may be faithful in attending church and presuming to serve God, may be blind. We may yet be guilty of sin by being blind—blind to the world as God sees it, blind to the work of God, and blind to the will of God.

BLIND TO THE WORLD AS GOD SEES IT

Those being appointed as missionaries are preparing to go to the ends of the earth because they have seen the world as God sees it. They have seen the spiritual darkness of the Muslim world where people are zealous to serve a distant and impersonal God but have no assurance of salvation. They have seen the hopelessness and despair of atheistic humanism across Western Europe and the former communist world and God's longing to draw them into a saving relationship with Him. They have seen the emptiness and futility of oriental philosophies, of those in bondage to African superstitions and fetishes, of multitudes in Latin America that are enslaved in Catholic ritualism—all who need to be delivered by a saving faith in Jesus Christ.

Because they see the world as God sees it, they have offered their lives to open blind eyes, to turn people from darkness to light and from the power of Satan to God. They have heard God pleading to "turn to Me and be saved, all the ends of the earth" (Isa. 45:22) and realized people cannot be saved if they don't believe. They cannot believe if they haven't heard, and they cannot hear unless you are willing to go and tell them.

Whenever I travel overseas, I am struck by an obvious contrast. On one hand it is thrilling to see the gospel taking root, churches being planted, and the kingdom of God growing. However, these results are often miniscule in the midst of massive cities and population groups. Last month I traveled throughout the Balkans and distributed Bibles in Muslim villages in Bosnia with our personnel there. I saw the lostness of those held in the stronghold of Orthodox traditions in Greece and Serbia. I gathered with our missionaries in Western Europe, a region that is actually regressing on our scale of evangelism. One cannot have these experiences and remain blind to the needs of a lost world.

One of you being appointed mentioned being led of God to pray for the nations of the world, particularly places where believers were being persecuted. But God convicted you to pray not so much for the persecuted but for the persecutors; they were the ones God wanted to reach. Your heart was changed as the Holy Spirit enabled you to see these people through His eyes.

But there are others who are still blind to a lost world. We quote proudly John 3:16 from an egocentric perspective, grateful that God loves us and has saved us. But when we read, "For God loved the world," that is not just our world of beautiful homes, well-appointed offices, manicured lawns, and shopping malls. We need to open our blind eyes to 1.7 billion people who have not even heard the name of Jesus. We need to open our blind eyes to starving refugees in Sudan and West Africa fleeing persecution and political oppression. We need to see a world victimized by war and ethnic conflicts, traumatized by earthquakes, floods, and natural disasters and realize God has called us to be a channel of His love and compassion and bring hope through Jesus Christ. Until we see the world as God sees it, our myopic and egocentric sin remains.

BLIND TO THE WORK OF GOD

Many are also blind to the work of God in the world today. But those of you being appointed have seen how God is at work. Your eyes have been opened to the way He is breaking down barriers that have prohibited religious freedom and proclamation of the gospel. He is using wars, chaos, social upheaval, and political disruption to turn the hearts of people to spiritual answers. Last year alone, 137 new unreached people groups heard the gospel for the first time. Our missionaries have been reporting an average of more than a thousand new believers a day being baptized for the last five years. That is not happening because of our mission strategies or clever programs. It is the power and providence of God moving to fulfill His purpose.

God is calling His people in record numbers, but it is not coincidental to what He is doing throughout the world as He opens doors that have been closed for generations, breaks down barriers to the gospel, and accelerates the harvest. We can't identify where most missionaries being appointed are going to serve because they have found creative ways to gain access to places restricted to a traditional missionary witness. They are willing to take the risks and plant their lives among unreached people groups and societies that are hostile to a Christian witness because they realize that Jesus is the answer and their eyes have been opened to see how God is at work throughout the Muslim world in Northern Africa and the Middle East. Their eyes have been opened to a church growth movement in China that is unprecedented since New Testament days that has drawn up to a hundred million people into the kingdom. Their eyes have seen the hand of God at work to open the former Soviet Union, Eastern Europe, and Central Asia to the gospel.

Those being appointed have had their eyes opened to the work of God, and they are going to join Him in His work. You realize it is not about your abilities and skills, but it is your availability to be used by the power of His Spirit. Our IMB vision statement says that "we will lead Southern Baptists to be on mission with God to bring all the peoples of the world to saving faith in Jesus Christ." We recognize it is not our mission, but God's. He is simply calling us to open our eyes and join Him in the task where He is at work until every knee shall bow and every tongue confess that Jesus is Lord. Many of God's people remain in sin and are disobedient to His call because they do not see how He is at work and are unwilling to join Him in His work.

BLIND TO THE WILL OF GOD

While many may be blind to the world and blind to the work of God, our greatest sin may be our blindness to the will of God. To those being appointed, your eyes have been opened to the will of God calling you to unlikely places like China, Russia, Indonesia, Uganda, Spain, Morocco, and Peru. You are going to places where it is dangerous to share a Christian witness, places where health and sanitation cannot be taken for granted and your children are likely to be deprived of normal social outlets. You would not be choosing to plant your lives in such places due to an arbitrary decision or out of a desire for personal success and recognition. No, you are going because of a compelling sense that it is God's will for you to go and do what you are going to do.

Did God choose you to be the one to dare to go into a Muslim culture with the gospel of Christ, to live in the desolate outback of West Africa or be overwhelmed by the congestion of a massive Asian city out of punishment for your past or because you have no usefulness in American society? No, it is because you are being given the privilege of sharing the good news of Christ with those who have never heard. It is because you have opened your eyes to see God's will, and He will reward you for your obedience.

Some of you began to discern God's will as a young person or student; you realized God had a special plan and purpose for your life, and it had something to do with fulfilling His mission to reach a lost world. For many of you, your blind eyes were opened on a short-term assignment or volunteer mission trip. When you saw the lostness and need, your eyes were opened to the potential within your own life of making a difference, and here you are, preparing to go.

A factor common to all in opening eyes that were once blind to God's will was that point in which God called you into submission to His lordship. You had first to lay your life on the altar and say, "Wherever You lead I'll go." Only then could God open your eyes to see His will, not your own. You see, most of you, like many others, are blinded to God's will by a commitment to personal plans and what you wanted to do. Many have chosen to see life in terms of their choice of professions, fulfilling their own interests, living for comforts and success. Like the Pharisees, they think they see, while they are actually blind to God's will. And like the Pharisees, our sin remains when we fail to open our eyes to what God would have us to do.

As you go to plant your life and witness to a lost world, we are grateful that your eyes were open to see God's will; your eyes were open to see a world in need and to see how God is at work, and you were willing to respond and say, "Here I am. Send me" (Isa. 6:8).

22

The Fear of the Lord

Psalm 25:12–14

Those of you being appointed to missionary service are surely excited about all that is in store for you as you anticipate going to serve as missionaries in the place to which God has called you. You are being dispersed to a variety of places all over the globe, and you go in confidence that God goes with you. You know there will be challenges, but you go willingly in anticipation of what God is going to do through you to reach an unreached people group or join missionary colleagues in a growing harvest. While you are confident of your call and secure in your faith, you likely feel a tinge of anxiety and concern about what you will encounter and whether or not you will be up to the task.

You probably realize that you are going to need wisdom and discernment to make cross-cultural adjustments, learn the language, and communicate the gospel effectively. You probably are concerned about your health and safety, going to places where neither can be taken for granted. We live in a world that is hostile to our Christian witness and increasingly adversarial to Americans presuming to share their faith where it is not welcome. We have intensified training in crisis contingencies, something which is more and more a relevant part of preparation to go overseas. You will be given a sufficient level of support because of the faithfulness of Southern Baptists to give to the Cooperative Program and Lottie Moon Christmas Offering, but you may have concerns for the needs of your family being met, wondering what kind of housing will be provided and how extensive the sacrifices will have to be in impoverished economies where there are no Walmarts. You are justified in wondering if you are spiritually adequate for the challenges and how you can walk with God, know His will, and follow His guidance with absolute assurance.

These are all areas of concern to Christians anywhere, but especially on the mission field. However, it is amazing that the Bible gives us a simple, singular condition that will assure all these needs and concerns are met. It is the way to know God's unquestioning will. It gives wisdom for all of life's choices. It is a guarantee of God's power, His blessing, provision for every need, and protection from danger. It is the basis for your success. In fact, it provides an abiding intimacy with the Father and access to the heart of God. It is what Jesus Himself valued above everything else.

Isaiah's prophecy in chapter 11, verses 1–4, is in reference to the coming of Jesus, the Messiah, who would descend from the root of Jesse. The Scripture says, "The Spirit of the LORD will rest on Him—a Spirit of wisdom and understanding, a Spirit of counsel and strength, a Spirit of knowledge and of the fear of the LORD. His delight will be in the fear of the LORD" (Isa. 11:2–3). God's Spirit provides knowledge to be informed, to know the issues and comprehend your situation. He gives understanding or insight to discern and perceive what you observe—how to put things in perspective. He gives wisdom to discern options, and the rationale for a course of action and counsel or guidance in the how-to or process of carrying on His mission and His work. And He also gives the courage and strength needed to accomplish the task that God sets before you. But notice, of all these things, "His delight will be in the fear of the LORD" (Isa. 11:3).

Most Christians would consider it strange that we are to fear the Lord. Our perception is that we shouldn't be afraid of God. He is a loving Father who delights to show mercy. We have an image of a compassionate shepherd, gently leading and nurturing us, His sheep. We have experienced His grace and cherish a personal relationship with Him that is a source of blessing, peace, and joy. What does it mean to fear the Lord?

It is difficult to make an appropriate analogy, but I think this is somewhat like the relationship I had with my parents. They loved me, cared for me, and were devoted to providing for my needs, and I recognized their authority over me. There was a respect for them that motivated my obedience and desire to behave in a way that pleased them. I knew if I disobeyed them or did something wrong I would be punished, but my fear of them was not fear of punishment. After all, the pain of a spanking was short-lived; I loved them and respected them, and that was a strong deterrent to disobedience.

We are called to stand in awe of a holy and righteous God who has called us to holiness and obedience. Yes, He does assure us that there are consequences of our sin and disobedience, and one day we will stand before Him and give an account of what we have done in this life, but that is not why we should fear Him. To fear the Lord means to have an awe-filled, holy reverence for Him, recognizing His lordship and that He has absolute authority over our life. The fear of the Lord is what brings us into willing submission to His will and elicits heartfelt praise and worship. It is recognizing that He alone is worthy of glory and honor. My study Bible describes the fear of the Lord as (1) a reverential awe, (2) obedient respect, and (3) a worshipful submission.

We have obviously lost the fear of God in our society and even in many of our churches. A lot of our conflicts would vanish if we allowed a fear of the Lord to subjugate our tendency of self-serving opinions and sense of entitlement to God's expectation that we would die to self and devote ourselves to serving others. We would be more conscientious about a holy lifestyle and faithfully witnessing of God's grace if we were overwhelmed by a fear of the Lord. And, I dare say, many more than these being appointed would be willing to offer their lives to fulfill our Great Commission task and go to the ends of the earth to share the gospel if we had a heart-convicting, life-controlling, vision-driven fear of the Lord!

The Fear of the Lord Puts You in a Proper Relationship with God

Proverbs 9:10 says, "The fear of the LORD is the beginning of wisdom, and the knowledge of the Holy One is understanding." All the sophisticated rationalization and wisdom of the world are misleading and a pretense. One does not have wisdom to deal with all the issues of life until one comes into a relationship of reverential awe and submission to God.

The fear of the Lord is the only real deterrent to moral failure. We have struggled with what we could do to intensify the screening process or do more in orientation that would absolutely guarantee no missionary would succumb to moral failure. Proverbs 16:6 tells us, "One turns from evil by the fear of the LORD." The only deterrent is to have a heart that is so desperate for God that we walk in obedient respect for His holiness and a desire to glorify Him; it is the fear of God that puts a hedge against sin around us.

Also, that relationship of fear and worshipful submission brings your life into focus, aligned with the purpose of God. Psalm 60:4 says, "You have given a signal flag to those who fear You." Can't you just picture medieval knights riding into battle with their banners flying? That banner represented the cause of their king—the purpose for which they devoted their lives. You will likely find yourself living for yourself, devoted to your own plans and desires, until the fear of the Lord brings you into submission to His purpose and plan for your life. The fear of the Lord gives you a banner—something worth living for.

THE FEAR OF THE LORD BECOMES A CHANNEL FOR GOD TO ACT IN YOUR LIFE

I dare say, everything that you want God to do for you comes about when relationship with Him is characterized by godly fear, awe, and respect. If you are going to a dangerous assignment and yearn for God's protection, Psalm 34:7 says, "The angel of the LORD encamps around those who fear Him."

If you want assurance of God's guidance, leading you, revealing His will, and watching over your every step, Psalm 33:18 says, "Now the eye of the LORD is on those who fear Him."

You will need courage. In times of discouragement and self-doubt when your witness is not bearing fruit and you begin to question God's call and are tempted to return home, Proverbs 14:26 reminds us, "In the fear of the LORD one has strong confidence."

You may be concerned about your needs being met in a place where there is no Walmart or familiar grocery products. You may be going to a place where you will not have social outlets for your family, and health and sanitation cannot be taken for granted. But the Lord will supply your need. Psalm 111:5 tells us, "He has provided food for those who fear Him." And Psalm 34:9 assures us, "Fear the LORD, you His saints, for those who fear Him lack nothing." The fear of the Lord opens the door for God to meet your needs, and who is more adequate, more sufficient, for all we need than Him?

THE FEAR OF THE LORD MUST BECOME THE SINGLE, DRIVING PASSION OF YOUR LIFE

If this is the key to God's blessing and power, the assurance of God's protection, God's provision and God's guidance, the key to wisdom and holiness, then we should be conscientious every day about walking in the fear of the Lord. It should become the passion and priority of our lives. Psalm 86:11–12 puts this in perspective: "Teach me Your way, LORD, and I will live by Your truth. Give me an undivided mind to fear Your name. I will praise You with all my heart, Lord my God, and will honor Your name forever." Isn't that what you want to happen when you get to the mission field—for the Lord to teach you His way, that you will walk in His truth and that your life and ministry will be to His praise and glory? Then your heart needs to be focused and unified on standing before Him in awe and fear of His name. Some Bible versions translate this, "Give me singleness of heart to fear your name." Don't let anything distract you from that. Don't allow the affections of your heart to be shared with anything and anyone, or allow anything to infringe upon this one, single priority of fearing the Lord.

But there is a bonus—an extra blessing when you come into such a relationship with God. Psalm 25:12–13 says, "Who is the person who fears the LORD? He will show him the way he should choose. He will live a good life, and his descendents will inherit the land." Now here is the clincher: "The secret counsel of the LORD is for those who fear Him, and He reveals His covenant to them" (Ps. 25:14). Isn't that awesome? Not only will God teach and guide you in His way, and prosper you and your descendants with blessings that you cannot imagine, He reveals His secrets to those who fear Him. That speaks of an intimate relationship in which you experience the spiritual depths of a relationship that brings you in touch with the heart of God.

I once heard a preacher speaking on this kind of relationship and intimacy with God, and he described it as "the expulsive power of a new affection." When you have the fear of God that brings you into a relationship with Him that is characterized by a reverential awe, an obedient respect and worshipful submission, you will find it expelling everything in your life that should not be there. You will find your love and fear of God eliminating everything that does not bring glory to Him. Every child of God should have that desire, and that's certainly where you want to be as you go to serve Him around the world.

23

Look, Love, and Live

1 John 3:17

Each one appointed to missionary service comes from a unique background with a diversity of gifts and experience. In God's providence each of you were privileged to come into a saving relationship with Jesus Christ, and through various circumstances He gave you a heart for a lost world and a passion to do something about it.

The Great Commission became personal as you realized the command of Christ to make disciples of all nations was not limited to a handful of disciples on a hillside in Galilee; although the Great Commission may be a generic mandate for the church, God made it personal and stirred your heart to realize the potential in your life to make a difference in a lost world. You have turned your back on success by promising to share hope with a people in darkness. You are moving beyond serving a local Stateside church to pursue something far more significant—God's glory among the nations.

Because most of us are staying here, where we live in the United States, we see your commissioning in terms of going. You are leaving your family and a familiar environment to go to a foreign country. Jesus commanded us to go, and that is what you are doing in obedience to His will. But I want to remind you that the command to go was not the first command of Jesus to those who chose to follow Him. It was not even a command to witness, to teach, or to baptize. The first imperative word of Jesus we find in the Gospels, after calling His disciples to follow, was the command to look.

THE COMMAND TO LOOK

Following His encounter with the woman at the well in the fourth chapter of John, Jesus said to His disciples, "Don't you say, 'There are still four more months, then comes the harvest'? Listen [to what] I'm telling you: Open your eyes and look at the fields, for they are ready for harvest" (John 4:35). Before you will ever be effective in your witness and fulfilling your mission call, you must see the world as God sees it. You must lift up your eyes to see the lostness and the potential harvest that is waiting.

Everyone has their own cultural worldview that is quite ethnocentric. One of our personnel serves in Nakus in northwest Uzbekistan among the Karakalpak people where he teaches in a technical school. He said this institution, in this very remote area of Central Asia, had a school song in which the lyrics described their school as the center of Nakus; Nakus is the center of Karakalpak Land, Karakalpak Land is the center of Uzbekistan, and Uzbekistan is the center of the world. It has never occurred to us that Uzbekistan is the center of the world because that is not our world. We tend to think the world centers around us, and, indeed, our world does. We see things from the perspective of our agenda, our lives, our families, and our needs. We see things from the perspective of Americans. We choose not to see the genocide in Darfur because it has nothing to do with us and our lifestyle. We do not see the unreached people groups who have never heard the gospel; they are irrelevant to us because they are far away from our realm of daily activities. But if we are to fulfill God's mission, we have got to open our eyes to see the world that God sees.

All you have to do is turn on your television newscast to see a world in war and turmoil, in hopelessness and despair. Jesus wants us to see the spiritual darkness of one billion Muslims, zealous in their faith and devotion, but without Christ. He wants us to lift our eyes and see 1.3 billion people who are isolated culturally and geographically in places where they have not even heard the name of Jesus. He wants us to see the multitudes of Hindus still bowing before lifeless idols. Jesus would say to open your eyes and see the Buddhists of Asia striving for enlightenment through their own futile efforts of accumulating karma by good works and to see a massive postmodern generation in Europe and across the world who are deluded into embracing humanistic beliefs of self-sufficiency without God.

Those of you being appointed as missionaries obeyed Jesus' command to look, and you have seen a lost world. You have been on short-term mission trips and have seen the need. But He also wants us to lift our eyes to see not only the lostness of the multitudes but also the fields that are white unto harvest. God is moving as never before through global events of political disruption, social upheaval, wars, and natural disasters to turn the hearts of people to spiritual answers that only Jesus can provide. Open your eyes, look beyond the headlines, and see a world in which God is at work among fields white unto harvest.

THE COMMAND TO LOVE

After Jesus commanded His disciples to look, He still did not follow with the command to go, but a subsequent imperative we find in His teachings was the command to love. Each of the Synoptic Gospels records the account of a Pharisee asking Jesus which was the greatest commandment. His reply was to quote Deuteronomy 6:5, "'Love the Lord your God with all your heart, with all your soul, and with all your mind.' . . . The second is like it: 'Love your neighbor as yourself'" (Matt. 22:37, 39). Earlier, as Jesus was preparing His followers for His crucifixion and death and the time He would leave them in the world to carry on His work, He said, "I give you a new commandment: love one another. Just as I have loved you, you must also love one another" (John 13:34).

Many have linked this with our mission task to point out that we have both a Great Commission in Matthew 28:19–20 and a Great Commandment in John 13:34. And you do not carry out one without the other. You will not be willing to go on behalf of God unless you love Him with all your heart. You will not give your life to extending His kingdom by doing whatever it takes to win and disciple the nations if you are not motivated by a passionate love for God and desire for Him to be glorified among all peoples.

But that love for God is seen and expressed in our love for others. It's easy to love our family and friends, but it is sometimes a challenge to love those even within our church fellowship when differences and conflicts arise. And we certainly are not reaching out and giving of ourselves to coworkers and others in our neighborhood out of a selfless love. However, Jesus followed this command with the story of the Good Samaritan to make clear that our neighbors we are to love are not just those who are like us. We are to love those who are different racially and culturally and even have antagonistic attitudes toward us.

When we glibly quote John 3:16 as a reminder that "God so loved the world," we need to understand that that is not just our world of comfortable suburban homes, well-appointed offices, a world of expressways and shopping malls. It is the world of impoverished refugees in the horn of Africa; it is the war-torn world of Sunnis, Shiites, and Kurds in Iraq. It is the famine and drought-stricken world of the Tuareg and Sokoto-Fulani of West Africa. Our neighbors are the millions suffering hopelessly in spiritual darkness around the world. God loves them and has commanded us to love them because His Son died for them. But without love, it is unlikely you would be willing to go. Giving of your life to God's mission call is meaningless if it is not motivated by His love for the nations.

THE COMMAND TO LIVE

Jesus commanded us to look—to see the fields that are white unto harvest. If we are to fulfill His calling and mission, we must see a lost world and see that God is at work. He commanded us to love God and to love that lost world because that is what will motivate us to give of ourselves. Yet He still did not command us to go but to live a life of love. Throughout His ministry He was teaching His disciples to embrace a new way of living, not the legalistic ritual imposed by their Jewish background, but they were to follow His commandments in spirit and truth. They were to abide in Him and reflect a Christlikeness of holiness and love. And as they lived out this new life in Christ, wherever they found themselves they were to make disciples and lead others to become followers of Christ. Wherever Christ led them, whether in Jerusalem and Judea where they lived or in their travels across the border into Samaria, or even to the ends of the earth, they were to be witnesses.

Most of us are familiar with the grammatical structure of the Great Commission and know the only active, imperative verb in this passage is not "to go," but it is "make disciples." Literally, Jesus said, "As you go," implying as they go about living for Him, wherever they may find themselves, they were to make disciples. He did not command them to go; it was an expectation. We are not to go to the ends of the earth because we are commanded to and someone has got to do it. If we look and see a lost world and obey His command to love that world, then we will be doing something to reach them and bring them into the kingdom.

You are going to fill a variety of assignments. Some of you will be in business support services. Others will be doing relief and development work, teaching English, engaged in medical work, or producing media resources. Wherever you are and whatever you are doing, the way you live must reflect the reality of Christ in you; otherwise, efforts to witness and persuade people of the truth of the gospel will have little effect. After Jesus told His disciples to love one another, He added, "By this all people will know that you are My disciples, if you have love for one another" (John 13:35). Never forget that is what will earn you a hearing among those who are hostile to the gospel; the way you live will give credibility to your verbal witness. It is what we call an incarnational witness—living out in flesh and blood the reality of the gospel.

So God is leading you to go. You have been obedient to His call to follow wherever He leads and to plant your life among those He wants to draw to Himself. But don't forget that your going is not in itself the essence of obedience to God's will. Jesus commanded you to look, to love, and to live out the gospel as you go.

Finally, consider our text—a very convicting verse found in 1 John 3:17 that says, "If anyone has this world's goods and sees his brother in need but shuts off his compassion from him—how can God's love reside in him?" This verse confronts us with four compelling questions.

The first is, "What do you have?" Do you have this world's goods? You may have trouble paying your bills to sustain an indulgent lifestyle and making your paycheck reach the end of the month, but relative to the suffering and poverty of our world, we have to admit that we have this world's goods. But we also have something else.

We have Jesus. We have been incredibly blessed to have salvation, something most of the world doesn't have; that is the greatest good one can have in this world.

The next question is, "What do you see?" Do you behold your brother in need? Are you willing to look beyond your self-centered concerns and ambition to see people in need—to see multitudes living a lifetime, dying and going to hell without Christ?

This leads to the obvious question that follows, "What do you give?" Or do you close your heart of compassion toward them, reasoning it doesn't concern you; they aren't your responsibility. You answer this question each time you give your mission offering, when you don't take time to pray for the nations and peoples of the world, or when you consider giving your life to go?

We need to understand that all of these questions are answered by the fourth question—"How much do you love?" For if we have what the world needs, if we see others who are lost and don't respond, then John concludes, "How does the love of God abide in you?"

24

Jesus Is Your Mission

1 Corinthians 2:1–5

Being appointed to missionary service is a significant milestone and time of transition in your life. It is the culmination of a journey that began when God called you to Himself, and you made a life-changing decision to place your faith in Jesus Christ as your Lord and Savior. The Bible reveals that, even before you were born, God knew you and had a plan and purpose for your life. He has found your heart sensitive to seek His will, and when He began to reveal that He had a place for you overseas, He found an obedient response. While this has been a long journey for some, for others it has been a short pilgrimage since God called you to put your personal plans aside and to lay on the altar your vocation and visions of a comfortable American lifestyle to reach a lost world.

You now face an unknown future of cross-cultural adjustments, learning to communicate in a new language and a journey of faith in which you rightfully expect God to provide for your every need. You still face a time of orientation and training before an airline ticket is placed in your hand and you leave for your country of assignment.

The training you will receive is focused around seven dimensions. Your time in orientation will include moving to a new level of discipleship, learning to be a team player, and preparing your family for adjustment to a foreign setting. You will receive training in cross-cultural witness and communication, how to be a mobilizer and to facilitate church-planting movements. You will be exposed to a broad spectrum of strategies and methodologies, and while all that is valuable, it is important to recognize that Jesus is the heart of your mission. The reason you are going overseas instead of serving God here in the States is simply because people are lost and need Jesus. Each of you has a unique assignment that fits your experience and skills, but your mission is not about filling a job description. It is not about responding to an urgent personnel request; it is primarily about taking Jesus to a lost world.

Dr. Tom Elliff, our senior vice president for Spiritual Nurture and Church Relations, recently returned from a conference with Russian pastors. One expressed appreciation for the conference materials with an ambiguous statement. He said, "Back during the days of the Soviet Union, there was oppression and persecution, and all we had was Jesus. It was a matter of knowing God or dying. Now with all the programs and strategies leaders from the West are bringing and teaching us, it is as if Jesus were not enough." You will find a great deal of value in learning certain skills, programs, and methodologies for cross-cultural witness and church planting, but never forget your mission is actually very pure and simple—Jesus is your mission.

JESUS IS YOUR MISSION

Jesus said in John 14:6, "I am the way, the truth, and the life. No one comes to the Father except through Me." In John 12:32, He said, "If I am lifted up from the earth I will draw all [people] to

Myself." I have always naïvely accepted that whatever the Bible says is true, and I get excited when Jesus said He will draw all men to Himself. However, that is contingent on His being lifted up from the earth. He was lifted up on the cross and purchased redemption for the whole world so that whoever calls on Him will be saved. He was lifted up from the earth as He ascended to the Father so that the Holy Spirit would come and empower us to be witnesses to the ends of the earth. But if all men—all peoples—are to be drawn to Jesus, we must lift Him up in a bold, positive witness before a lost world.

I can remember my first few months on the field following language study. I was diligently seeking to implement all I had learned in seminary and orientation and do what I had seen veteran missionary colleagues doing, but I was not seeing results. I was getting frustrated and discouraged as all my efforts were met with indifference, and even antagonism, among the Muslim people in Indonesia. In despondency I fell on my face, angry at God because He was not keeping His part of the bargain. I had committed my life, left the potential of a comfortable and successful ministry in the States; I expected Him to empower and bless my work, and He wasn't doing it. In that time of crisis, He led me back to the book of Acts where multitudes of believers were coming to faith every day. As I read the Scripture, I realized what these "ignorant and unlearned" disciples of Jesus were doing—as the Bible described them. They were simply proclaiming Jesus in a bold, positive witness.

Jesus is your mission. Do you remember the testimony of the men on the road to Emmaus in Luke 24:31? The Scripture says, "Their eyes were opened, and they recognized Him." What you want to happen as you go to India, Western Europe, the Middle East, Africa, and Latin America is that the eyes of the people would be opened to recognize Jesus. They don't know that He is what they are looking for as they go through meaningless religious ritual or as they succumb the futile self-sufficiency of secular humanism. But they are reflecting the attitude of the Greeks who came to Philip saying, "Sir, we want to see Jesus" (John 12:21).

Jesus Is the Message of Your Mission

Realize that Jesus is not only the objective and essence of your mission; He is the message of your mission. This was the message of the apostles. They declared in Acts 4:12, "There is salvation in no one else; for there is no other name under heaven given to people by which we must be saved." A postmodern world resents such a narrow, absolute perspective. They would have us believe it really doesn't matter what one believes—that all religions, and even good works, eventually lead to God. It appears to be arrogant and condescending to say that Jesus is the only way. But that is your message. You are not called to proclaim a politically correct message or to compromise the gospel to make it palatable to your audience.

The death, burial, and resurrection of the Son of God is the only provision for redeeming a lost world from the sin that separates them eternally from a holy and righteous God; therefore, it is the message of your mission. We read of the new believers in Acts 5:42, that "every day in the temple complex, and in various homes, they continued teaching and proclaiming the good news that the Messiah is Jesus." Just as they gathered for one purpose—to teach and preach Jesus—He is the message of your mission as well.

Paul, in writing to the church at Corinth, confessed his inadequacy and revealed the key to his effectiveness. "When I came to you, brothers, announcing the testimony of God to you, I did not come with brilliance of speech or wisdom. . . . And I was with you in weakness, in fear, and in much trembling. My speech and my proclamation were not with persuasive words of wisdom, but with a demonstration of the Spirit and power, so that your faith might not be based on men's wisdom but on God's power"

(1 Cor. 2:1, 3–5). Now you may be somewhat disillusioned to hear that. Perhaps you have had the image of Paul as such an effective evangelist who was eloquent in speech, bold in his witness, able to skillfully weave persuasive arguments to convince people of the truth of the gospel. To the contrary, he did not see himself as eloquent in the language. He stood before people with butterflies in his stomach, scared to death, just as you will. But he said in verse 2, "For I determined to know nothing among you except Jesus Christ and Him crucified." We are hopeful that you are going to develop an adequate level of fluency in the language, but you, too, will be overwhelmed by the cultural barriers and struggle to explain the gospel in the context of other worldviews. You will be terrified as you seek to witness in places where people don't welcome your Christian testimony. Just remember, it is not about you; Jesus is your message.

JESUS IS THE MEANS OF YOUR MISSION

Jesus is not only your mission and the message of your mission; He is also the means of fulfilling your mission. As Jesus was moving toward His crucifixion and was preparing His disciples to continue His ministry, He reminded them, "I am the vine; you are the branches. The one who remains in Me and I in him produces much fruit, because you can do nothing without Me" (John 15:5). Paul acknowledged this when he testified of having preached the gospel from Jerusalem to Illyricum. He said it wasn't what he did, but "by the power of miraculous signs and wonders, and by the power of God's Spirit." He said, "I would not dare say anything except what Christ has accomplished through me to make the Gentiles obedient by word and deed" (Rom. 15:18–19).

You will write newsletters back to your family and friends. You will report to your church about your ministry and activities. But there is nothing worth speaking of except what Christ does through you to bring the nations and peoples of the world to faith. That is what Christ is seeking to do through all of us. It is not your ability but your availability to Him and the power of His Spirit that will fulfill your mission. It could not be stated more clearly than in Galatians 2:19–20: "I have been crucified with Christ; and I no longer live, but Christ lives in me. The life I now live in the flesh, I live by faith in the Son of God, who loved me and gave Himself for me."

As you go to the mission field, realize that Jesus is the means of fulfilling your mission. May your passion and desire be that expressed by Paul, "[My goal] is to know Him and the power of His resurrection and the fellowship of His sufferings" (Phil. 3:10). Paul was convinced that Jesus was the power and means for whatever God called him to do for he said, "I am able to do all things through Him who strengthens me" (Phil. 4:13).

JESUS IS THE MAJESTY OF YOUR MISSION

Not only is Jesus your mission, the message of your mission, and the means of your mission; He is the majesty of your mission. For as you go to lift up Jesus, proclaiming Him among the nations, we are assured that one day, "at the name of Jesus every knee should bow . . . and every tongue should confess that Jesus Christ is Lord, to the glory of God the Father" (Phil. 2:10–11). What a glorious day that will be when a Tuareg from West Africa, a Sudanese, perhaps touched by your witness in a European city, a Hazara from Afghanistan, and Kurdish believers from Turkey and Iraq all stand around the throne of God because you go in obedience to God's call.

But the reward and the glory will not be for your faithfulness in service or obedience to God's call; all the glory and majesty will go to the Lamb of God. We are told in Revelation, "You were slaughtered, and You redeemed [people] for God by Your blood from every tribe and language and people and nation. . . . The Lamb who was slaughtered is worthy to receive power and riches and wisdom and strength and honor and glory and blessing! . . . forever and ever!" (Rev. 5:9, 12–13). Jesus is the majesty of your mission.

In conclusion, as you are reminded that Jesus is your mission, the message of your mission, the means of your mission, and the majesty of your mission, it is important that you heed the admonition of Hebrews 12:1–2: "Therefore since we also have such a large cloud of witnesses surrounding us, let us lay aside every weight and the sin that so easily ensnares us, and run with endurance the race that lies before us, keeping our eyes on Jesus, the source and perfecter of our faith, who for the joy that lay before Him endured a cross and despised the shame, and has sat down at the right hand of God's throne." Keep your eyes on Jesus as you run the race.

25

The Pattern of a Missionary Witness

Acts 14

I have often shared that when I went to Indonesia as a new missionary in 1970 I expected the pages of Acts to unfold with multitudes being saved every day. Never mind that this was the largest Muslim country in the world and people were largely indifferent to the gospel and even antagonistic to a Christian witness. Although I was somewhat naïve, my enthusiasm and vision were not unmerited.

After all, the Bible does reveal God's plan and desire to bring all the peoples of the earth to saving faith in Jesus Christ. He made clear that the gospel was the power of God to bridge that gap of sin and draw people to Himself. All that was lacking was an evangel, someone to go and tell them the good news of God's love and the way of redemption.

Jesus left the mandate with His followers that they were to be His witnesses to the ends of the earth, but He instructed them to wait in Jerusalem until they were endued with power from on high. Soon that time came as the Holy Spirit empowered their witness,

and the book of Acts tells us that three thousand people responded
and were baptized in one day. This initial harvest wasn't just among
local people in Jerusalem but included devout men from every nation
under heaven. Why would the apostles be so amazed? Didn't Jesus
tell them just a few days earlier that they were to disciple the nations?

From that moment there was no deterrent to the spread of the
gospel as the Lord continued to add to the number of believers on
a daily basis. In chapter 6 of Acts, we read that even Jewish priests
were becoming obedient to the faith; and in chapter 9, not only were
the believers multiplying, but the number of churches had begun to
multiply.

Just as Jesus outlined, the gospel permeated Jerusalem, spread
throughout Judea, and then began to bridge cross-culturally into
Samaria. Then we come to an interesting transition in God's plan
for global evangelism. It was time for the gospel to explode out of
that narrow Jewish context and geographic confinement and spread
to the ends of the earth. God converted and called a Jewish rabbi
named Paul to begin the process, and it is the same reason He has
called you today.

Paul had a vision to go to the regions beyond; he had a passion that
those who had never heard the gospel would hear and understand.
He developed a "wigtake" attitude—whatever it's going to take—to
get the gospel to all peoples. He would never have imagined that
those of you today would be going to remote people groups in South
America, Africa, Central Asia, and China. But he set a pattern that
you would do well to emulate.

In a short time, following a period of training and initial
language study and orientation, you will be going to places like
Indonesia, Peru, India, and Tanzania. Notice the pattern Paul set
of a missionary witness in Acts 14. In verse 1—"The same thing
happened in Iconium; they entered the Jewish synagogue and spoke
in such a way that a great number of both Jews and Greeks believed."

Isn't that what you want to happen—a multitude of people to believe? Note what we are told about why that happened.

SPEAK THE LANGUAGE OF THE PEOPLE

They spoke in such a manner that a great multitude believed. Obviously Paul had the advantage of using a common Greek language on his journeys, but you cannot expect people to understand and respond if you don't communicate the gospel in their language. On our first stateside assignment, I was demonstrating speaking in the Indonesian language among a group of young people, and one of them responded, "Why don't you teach them all English so you wouldn't have to learn and speak that language?" He obviously didn't comprehend there were 200 million Indonesians who have their own language!

One of your first tasks is learning the language, not just vocabulary and grammatical structures but how to communicate cross-culturally in the context of relationships and ways of thinking. That will be a continual process. You won't engage a year of formal language study and be done, but for the rest of your time on the field you will be learner. Not only will you be learning words but building relationships, identifying with the people that you might speak into their lives in a manner that would convince them of the truth of the gospel and draw them to Christ.

RELY ON THE LORD AND WITNESS BOLDLY

Just as opposition arose in Iconium, you will encounter opposition. Many of the places to which you are being appointed do not welcome a missionary presence, and the people are hostile to a Christian witness. It is not just a matter of religious differences, but your message will be a threat to their culture and way of life.

Does that mean you should be intimidated, cower in fear, opt for discretion, and dilute your message? No, we are told that Paul and his companions "stayed there for some time and spoke boldly, in reliance on the Lord" (Acts 14:3).

It wasn't their nature to take risks and ignore the danger. It wasn't human courage or foolishness that caused them to boldly confront opposition. Their boldness came from relying on the Lord. You have fulfilled various requirements of education, experience, and training, but you are never to rely on your own ability. God has promised to go with you and never to forsake you. Trust in Him for the courage and wisdom to proclaim the gospel.

In times of discouragement when I did not see a response to my witness, I tried all the methods and strategies I had learned to no effect. But as I read again through the book of Acts, I realized that what the apostles and early missionaries did was to faithfully lift up Jesus in a bold, positive witness. Acts 4:33 tells us, "And with great power the apostles were giving witness to the resurrection of the Lord Jesus." If you are to see response, you must rely on the Lord and witness boldly.

TRUST GOD FOR RESULTS

As they relied on the Lord and witnessed boldly, Acts 14:3 goes on to tell us that "the Lord . . . testified to the message of His grace by granting that signs and wonders be performed through them." It is not your words, fluency of language, and persuasive arguments that will convince people of the truth of the gospel. Paul confessed in 1 Corinthians 2:1–5 that "announcing the testimony of God" he "did not come with brilliance of speech or wisdom." He said, "I was with you in weakness, in fear, and in much trembling. My speech and my proclamation were not with persuasive words of wisdom." He went on to explain this was necessary so that their faith would not rest on the wisdom of men but on the power of God.

This doesn't mean that God is necessarily going to empower you to perform miracles, though our missionaries do occasionally testify to signs and wonders that can only be explained by God's sovereign power. I continue to be amazed at Muslims in Indonesia who would come to faith in Christ. They experienced opposition from their families, were ostracized from their community, sometimes lost their job, and even had their life threatened. Why would they turn their back on their religion, society, and culture and embrace a belief that had been introduced to them by a foreigner who could not even communicate fluently in their language. There is no explanation except the power of God that indwells the message of the gospel. Trust God to work through your witness.

DISCIPLE THE BELIEVERS

In Acts 14:22 we read that they were "strengthening the hearts of the disciples by encouraging them to continue in the faith." It is not enough just to witness and rejoice in the response; there is a responsibility to nurture new believers in the faith. It is not unlikely they will come under intense social pressure and be tempted to renounce their faith. You will have to deal with the tendency of syncretism in which they try to conform their new faith in Jesus Christ to their old religious concepts.

The people in Iconium and Lystra responded to the gospel, but they thought Paul and Barnabas were Jupiter and Mercury because their message and ministry seemed to fit the concepts they had of their pagan deities. You are going to people who have never had a Bible; they have no background whatsoever for understanding the plan of salvation. They may readily respond to a message that offers assurance of forgiveness of sin and eternal life, but they have to be taught the tenets of their faith and strengthened and encouraged that they might grow and stand firm in the face of tribulation.

AVOID DEPENDENCY, TRAIN THE LEADERS, AND IMPLEMENT AN EXIT STRATEGY

Paul had been in each of these cities only two or three weeks, but we read in verse 23, "When they had appointed elders for them in every church and prayed with fasting, they committed them to the Lord in whom they had believed." You are the one that is proclaiming the gospel. As believers respond, they will need to be taught and discipled. God will draw them together into a fellowship of believers to form a new church that will be an ongoing nucleus of witness in that location, but it must not become dependent on your leadership lest the congregation be handicapped from the beginning. Paul appointed or ordained elders—pastor leaders—in each place, not because they were so well-qualified but because he entrusted them to the Lord.

Confident that God will be faithful to give gifts to each new church for its needs and equipping, you are to move on, taking the gospel to other areas, pushing back the frontier of lostness. Go in with an exit strategy rather than staying too long and creating dependency on you instead of God.

FINALLY, COME BACK AND REPORT TO YOUR SENDING CHURCHES

You can begin to look forward to that. Paul and his team returned to Antioch, and when "they arrived and gathered the church together, they reported everything God had done with them, and that He had opened the door of faith to the Gentiles" (Acts 14:27). God has called you, and you have responded in obedience to the challenge of the Great Commission. Though the International Mission Board is appointing you and channeling your support, your accountability is to the churches that send you. They provide your support through the denomination and cooperative channels of giving. They will sustain you with their prayers. You are their missionaries.

After an initial term of three or four years, you will have the opportunity of returning on a stateside assignment. That is not a well-earned time of vacation but an opportunity to report to the churches how God strengthened you in times of trials, loneliness, and adjustments. You will tell about people who don't have the privilege of knowing God's love, and you will testify to the power of God drawing people to Himself because you went and served faithfully. It won't be about what you have done but what God has done through you for His glory among the nations.

That is a fairly precise outline of what you are going to do. As you are diligent in following Paul's pattern and relying on the Lord, you can expect, as he did, a great number of people to believe.

26

Retaining the Song

2 Chronicles 29:27

We have just completed a phenomenal week of fellowship with 1,150 emeritus missionaries. These men and women are our heroes. They are the model to which you as new missionaries aspire. They have served all over the world, many in pioneer areas that are now seeing a harvest of church growth. Global advance in missions today is built on the foundations they laid. We stand on their shoulders, praising God for their faithfulness and perseverance. Some of them represent more than forty years of tenure on the mission field. Assuming the average tenure of twenty-three years for missionaries who serve to retirement, they represent a cumulative twenty-six thousand years of missionary labor around the world.

We have heard a few of their testimonies. Some were blessed to see a harvest of souls and churches planted while many labored faithfully sowing the seed on resistant fields with a vision for that future day when the fruit would come. It wasn't an easy life, as they will all testify. There were hardships and trials. Many lost husbands, wives, or children to disease or tragic accidents. They were far away when loved ones in the States passed away. They struggled with the stress of government restrictions, religious opposition, deprived living conditions, and interpersonal conflicts. Yet they remained faithful and kept the song in their heart.

Have you had those days when everything was going right? You felt loved, appreciated, and valued. Bills were paid, the sun was shining, you felt blessed and sensed God's presence in your life. The lyrics of a familiar hymn or praise song was likely on your mind. The book of Psalms characterizes a proper relationship with God as a song. "Come, let us shout joyfully to the LORD, shout triumphantly to the rock of our salvation!" (Ps. 95:1). "Sing a new song to the LORD, for He has performed wonders" (Ps. 98:1). That song in our hearts and on our lips reflects a relationship with God in which all is well, our confidence is secure, and joy overflows.

But on other days the song is not there. Burdens and anxieties displace the joy. Difficulties and problems overwhelm you, and you feel that God is nowhere to be found. Faithless prayers seem hollow and perfunctory, and the witness of a victorious life is an illusion. I went through such cycles of emotion frequently on the mission field, just as these former missionaries did. I can remember times of discouragement when the children were sick, and we were harassed as foreigners in an unfamiliar culture. We were not seeing a response to our witness and felt God had let us down. The song turned to grumbling and complaining, and it was not unusual in such situations to think of giving up and going home. It's terrible to lose the song, the sense of God's presence and assurance of His blessing, and a victorious walk with Him. How do you keep from losing the song, or when you do, recover it? Vance Havner had a sermon on "Recovering the Song" based on 2 Chronicles 29:27. This verse reads, "Then Hezekiah ordered that the burnt offering be offered on the altar. When the burnt offerings began, the song of the LORD and the trumpets began." The point that he made was that the song is a result of the sacrifice being laid on the altar. What robs us of the song, a sense of well-being and relationship with God, is an attitude of entitlement or holding on to things and attitudes that must be relinquished in order to be set free to enjoy a victorious life.

You Have Been Called to Sacrifice Your Life

Some of you have left a successful business or professional career. Others are leaving an effective ministry as a pastor or church staff. Some of you, after years of education and training, have attained a comfortable and affluent lifestyle, have finally built your dream home, and are now leaving all in obedience to Christ's call. While you may have anxieties over the uncertainty of what you may face in cross-cultural adjustments on the mission field, you have joy in coming to this point of commitment. Being commissioned as a missionary culminates a pilgrimage of seeking and following God's will, and there is a joy in anticipation of how God is going to use you to touch a lost world.

Each of these emeritus missionaries' lives would testify to the truth of James 1:2, which tells us, "Consider it a great joy . . . whenever you experience various trials." That is why they persevered and endured difficulties that brought others home. They counted it joy to make the sacrifice, to bear the suffering and hardship, and in doing so they retained the song.

When we resent the sacrifice and don't want to give up things that have become of value, we are robbed of the song. It is not unusual for missionaries to engage in a pity party because their electricity goes off, and they can't enjoy their modern appliances. When the heat is stifling, the sewage backs up, and the car won't start, we think of how well we had it back in the States! You will never get the joy back and the song in your heart until you give it up and relinquish it to the Lord.

Paul said in Romans 12:1, "By the mercies of God, I urge you to present your bodies as a living sacrifice, holy and pleasing to God." No, just leaving America to go as a missionary to a foreign country is not enough. God expects you to lay on the altar your life and everything that you may be holding on to in terms of lifestyle and worldly goods. You have had sessions this week on packing your crate and are already facing the dilemma of what must be sold or given away among your household furnishings and precious goods. But as you go, heed the advice of Dr. Baker James Cauthen, former president who appointed us and many of those emeritus missionaries. He said, "Whatever you take with you, take in your hands and not in your heart."

You Are to Offer the Sacrifice of a Broken and Contrite Heart

You may think it is sufficient to sacrifice your life, your dreams, and personal ambition to go as a missionary, but it is not just a role that God has called you to fill. It is not enough to fill a job description and faithfully perform your task in places like Brazil, West Africa, India, or China. David discovered this, when, in his penitent Psalm 51, he expressed the desire to do whatever he could to please God. He came to the conclusion: "You do not want a sacrifice, or I would give it; You are not pleased with a burnt offering. The sacrifice pleasing to God is a broken spirit. God, You will not despise a broken and humbled heart" (Ps. 51:16–17).

Probably the worst thing you could take to the mission field would be a sense of self-sufficiency. After all, you have been educated and trained; you will go through additional orientation and training to prepare you for cross-cultural witness and ministry. You are mature and experienced. Obviously, God has called you because you are His gift to a lost world and just what they need! I think the greatest disillusionment I experienced upon arrival on the mission field was to be confronted with my own spiritual mediocrity. I was deeply convicted of my shallow faith and walk with the Lord. A successful Stateside pastorate and ministry had given me a sense of prideful confidence that I realized was detestable to God. Before I could be used of God, I had to fall on my face acknowledging my unworthiness, confessing my pride and brokenness over sin in my life. And I have found over the years that a broken and contrite heart is essential for restoring a proper relationship with God in which the flow of His grace and love brings the song to your heart.

That brokenness must not only be for your own sin, but you need to bring to God the sacrifice of a heart broken over the sins of a lost world. Psalm 126:5–6 tells us, "Those who sow in tears will reap with shouts of joy. Though one goes along weeping, carrying the bag of seed, he will surely come back with shouts of joy, carrying his sheaves." Nothing will bring a song to your heart more than winning the lost to Jesus. You may be in the throes of depression, and everything around you may be unraveling. That is probably evidence of succumbing to a self-centered attitude, as if it were all about you, your needs, and your comforts. What you need to do is get out and tell someone about Jesus. You will never retain the song on the mission field until your heart is broken and you care more for the lost around you than for your own comforts and convenience. Only those who sow in tears will reap with joy. There is no greater joy than being the one to tell someone about Jesus who has never heard. And you have that privilege. Offer God the sacrifice of a broken and contrite heart, and you will return with songs of joy, bearing sheaves of redeemed into the kingdom.

You Are to Offer the Sacrifice of Praise

Finally the Scripture indicates that we are to offer the sacrifice of praise. "Through Him let us continually offer up to God a sacrifice of praise, that is, the fruit of our lips that confess His name" (Heb. 13:15). The Bible tells us that God inhabits the praises of His people. That is why, if we want a sense of His presence each day, if we want assurance of His blessing being poured out to sustain us, strengthen us, and meet our every need, if we want to live with a song in our hearts, then we need to offer praise to Him continually, giving thanks for all things.

I learned why this is the key to victory over all the trials and disappointments one may face. When plans go awry, tragedy strikes your family, the work for which you labored disintegrates and falls apart, praise the Lord anyway. For when you praise the Lord, your attention is diverted from the situation and circumstances back to the Lord. And when your attention is focused on the Lord, you are reminded that He is with you. And when you become mindful that He is with you, He is able to take control of your attitude and put things in the perspective of God's providence and faithfulness to work in all things for our blessing and welfare and for His glory. Yes, it may be a challenge in the circumstances you are going through, but the key to victory is offering the sacrifice of praise. When the sacrifice is on the altar, the song of the Lord will begin.

Vance Havner concluded his message by observing many Christian workers have lost their song, just as many of those emeritus missionaries could testify of times they lost the song. In response, some resign and come home. Others become resigned to the situation and continue to go through the motions without any joy in their life or ministry. But others seek God's face, return to the altar of sacrifice, and they are re-"signed" to a relationship with God in which the Spirit flows with power and joy.

Jasper McPhail was our first Southern Baptist missionary to go to India. He was able to open medical work there because of his credentials as a cardiovascular surgeon, and a door of witness has continued to expand. As he left a very successful and lucrative medical practice in Memphis, Tennessee, to go as a missionary to India, people would ask him, "How can you give up and sacrifice all you have attained to go as a missionary?" Dr. McPhail replied, "What am I giving up? I gave up my life to do God's will when I trusted Him as my Savior. To sacrifice means to give up that which is of value in your life. That which is of greatest value to me is God's will and calling on my life. How could I consider it a sacrifice to go to India for Christ when He considered it a privilege to go to Calvary for me?"

27

Results of Obedience
to the Call

Exodus 19:3–6

Recently we recognized and honored more than sixty missionaries retiring from a lifetime of service overseas. They have witnessed many changes in the organization, structure, and mission strategy of the International Mission Board during their years of tenure, but they served faithfully and stayed focused on the unchanging task. Although they were returning home to the States after thirty to forty years of cross-cultural witness and ministry, they consider those places where they have planted their lives and raised their families as home. They will long for the familiar as they adjust to the hectic pace of life in the U.S. and having to live in a society that has changed radically since their departure years ago.

They mirror the career that you are just beginning as you leave America and prepare to identify with the people among other cultures to whom God has called you. You are going in obedience to God's call, and I pray that you will persevere and remain obedient to that call through the years of adversity and trials as you sow the seed and reap the harvest. Though these emeritus missionaries have brought closure to their overseas service, they will continue in witness and ministry wherever they are, for God's calling is irrevocable. Most significant, however, is the fact that the impact of their ministry on the mission field doesn't end with their retirement. It continues to multiply through the believers they led to the Lord and discipled to serve Him. The book doesn't close on their final statistical report, as the churches they planted will continue to bear witness and multiply long after their departure from the field. Only eternity will reveal the results of their obedience to the call.

I want to challenge those of you being appointed to fulfill the Great Commission mandate of our Lord to think in terms of what you can anticipate as a result of your obedience to God's call. You don't know how long you will have to serve overseas. Not all of you will be able to invest your life and serve until retirement. Health needs and family crisis will bring some of you home prematurely. In the dynamic of a changing world, some will be among those sensing a shift in God's leadership back to a Stateside ministry. But the future course of your life and ministry will be forever shaped by your obedience to God's call at this time and a heart for reaching a lost world.

A passage of Scripture that reflects the significance of your service is the experience of Moses on Mount Sinai in Exodus 19:3–6: "Moses went up [the mountain] to God, and the LORD called to him from the mountain: 'This is what you must say to the house of Jacob, and explain to the Israelites: You have seen what I did to the Egyptians and how I carried you on eagles' wings and brought you to Me. Now if you will listen to Me and carefully keep My covenant, you will be My own possession out of all the peoples, although all the earth is Mine, and you will be My kingdom of priests and My holy nation.'"

Like Moses, You Heard and Responded to God's Call

For some of you, it was many years ago when God spoke into your life and called you to be a missionary, but you clearly remember and can relate to that call many years later. Through various circumstances God planted the conviction that He was calling you personally to plant your life overseas and take the gospel to those who had never heard. For others, it might have been as a young person or college student seeking to know God's will that He impressed upon you the potential of your life to touch a lost world that needed to know Jesus. Many of you were already on another career track when God called you through a volunteer mission trip or hearing a speaker tell of the needs of a lost world, and you responded in obedience.

That call is still fresh and is being confirmed by your appointment tonight. Your experience may have been a mystical call or simply a convicting impression that you recognized as the still, small voice of God, but you gave yourself to a higher calling. Your response and focus on that call brought you into an intimate relationship with God, in which you sought His guidance and timing in the process. You stayed focused on what God had revealed to you, not as a unique encounter with Him as a point in time, but a continuing pilgrimage of walking with Him. In a sense, as with Moses, you heard God's call and went up on the mountain with Him.

You Will See the Mighty Works of God

In His conversation with Moses, God reminded him of three things He had done for His people Israel. First, He said, "You have seen what I did to the Egyptians and how I carried you on eagles' wings and brought you to Me." The children of Israel had witnessed the sovereign power of God delivering them from bondage in Egypt and then destroying the pursuing army of Pharaoh. Perhaps not in the same dramatic fashion, but you will have had the privilege of seeing the mighty hand of God work through the power of the gospel to bring people out of bondage to sin and into the kingdom of God. Many of you will serve in pioneer assignments where you will be the first evangelist to plant the seed of the gospel in a city or people group. You need to be aware that many of those emeritus missionaries testified that it was nothing they did but only the hand of God that saved people out of Buddhist cultures or empty ritualistic Catholic faith. They had the privilege of seeing Muslims confess Jesus as their Savior and Africans set free from bondage to their traditional superstitions and fears, only because they were witnesses of God's power.

Those retiring had the privilege of serving in an era of global advance and growth in which more than thirteen hundred new believers a day are being baptized. The number of new churches planted each year has grown from a few thousand to over twenty-three thousand last year. They have witnessed the power and providence of God using warfare, political upheaval, and natural disasters throughout the world to open doors of opportunity so that more than a hundred unreached people groups a year are being engaged with the gospel. That has not been so much a result of IMB strategy and their diligence and hard work as it has demonstrated the mighty works of God.

God is the One who called you to Himself and to His mission. He has promised to go with you and sustain you; He will bear you up as on eagles' wings. And you will have the privilege of seeing His mighty, miracle-working power just as real as His rolling back the waters of the Red Sea and delivering the children of Israel from bondage in Egypt.

You Will See God's Faithfulness in Caring for You

Not only will you see the mighty works of God, like each of those emeritus missionaries testified, but God will be faithful in caring for you as you go. God's reminder to Moses that He had borne them on eagles' wings, brings to mind the passage in Isaiah 40:31: "Those who trust in the LORD will renew their strength; they will soar on wings like eagles; they will run and not grow weary; they will walk and not faint." I won't go so far as to say you will not get weary, but you will experience God's strength and guidance. When difficulties and trials come, you will feel His hand lifting you and sustaining you through times of grief and heartache. When you encounter obstacles to your ministry, when you become discouraged and feel you cannot go on, you will find a renewal that comes from the Lord as He bears you up as on eagle's wings and meets your every need. His grace will be sufficient.

God Will Bring You into an Intimate Relationship with Him

You will be able to persevere and possibly serve to retirement because God will be constantly drawing you to Himself. There is no way you can stay on the field and make it all the way if you do not find a special relationship with God. You must meet Him each day in your quiet time of prayer and devotion. As your faith is strengthened by His Word, He will reveal Himself and unfold His will and plans for you to follow. When your spiritual walk becomes dry and your witness barren, God will draw you back into the source of strength in fellowship with Him. You will experience the reality of Psalm 91:1–2, "The one who lives under the protection of the Most High dwells in the shadow of the Almighty. I will say to the LORD, 'My refuge and my fortress, my God, in whom I trust.'"

Following these three affirming reminders, God makes an awesome promise to Moses and to the people. "If you will . . . carefully keep My covenant, you will be My own possession out of all the peoples, although all the earth is Mine, and you will be My kingdom of priests and My holy nation."

You Will Be God's Possession and Representative to Bring the Nations to Him

Because you are committed to keeping His covenant and are faithful and obedient to His calling, He is allowing you to be His representative among the peoples of the earth. Israel was called and chosen of God, not for their own blessing and benefit, but to be a kingdom of priests to declare His glory among the nations and His salvation to the ends of the earth. You are called to a priestly role, to stand in the gap between a lost world bound for hell and represent God's saving grace to bring people into the kingdom.

You are our heroes; we respect and honor you tonight for your obedience to God's call. But far greater than the esteem we have for you is the fact you are special to God. In places where His name is not known, where people are in darkness and, as Isaiah said, are not a people, you will be His possession, precious and holy. You have the privilege of fulfilling your priestly function to bring them to God as a part of His plan that one day every knee will bow and every tongue confess that Jesus is Lord to the glory of God the Father.

You will join a host of colleagues on the field as the ones to bring us closer to that day when those from every tribe, people, tongue, and nation will be gathered around the throne, worshipping the Lamb as God spoke here in Exodus when He said, "All the earth is Mine" (Exod. 19:5). How will all of this come about? It is because one day you said, like Israel, in response to Moses' words in Exodus 19:8, "We will do all that the LORD has spoken."

28

The Call of God

Exodus 3:9–12

If there is any verse of Scripture a good Southern Baptist knows, next to John 3:16, it would be the Great Commission in Matthew 28:19–20, where Jesus tells us to go into all the world and make disciples of all nations. However, we often rationalize that mandate of our Lord to make it apply to anything we happen to do in witness and ministry, ignoring the fact that the object is to proclaim the gospel to the ends of the earth. Many have excused themselves from any personal obligation by reasoning that only a select few are called by God to go as missionaries to the nations, and the rest of us are exempt and simply provide the support.

Often, after an appointment service or missions emphasis, someone will approach me and say, "Dr. Rankin, I would be willing to go as a missionary, but God has not called me." I have never figured out how to respond tactfully to that comment. I want to ask in response, "Do you have the same Bible I have? To whom do you think the Great Commission was given—just a handful of disciples on a hillside in Galilee? Or just an elite few among all of God's people?" The IMB now has fifty-three hundred missionary personnel serving overseas. That may sound like a lot, but it is only one missionary unit—family or single person—for almost each three million people.

Not only that, it represents only .03 percent of Southern Baptists—not even one out of every three thousand. The rest of us rationalize that unless God has confronted us with a burning bush or a mystical Damascus Road experience, we are exempt. I fail to understand how we have a God who yearns for the nations to know of His love and the fact that Jesus died for them, and here is a dedicated Christian who says I would even be willing to go, but I don't because God has chosen not to call me! We should not blame God for our failure to be obedient to the challenge of the Great Commission. No one is exempt from God's call and the responsibility to reach a lost world. It is not a matter of a dichotomy between those who are called and those who are permitted to stay at home but a matter of discovering our place in fulfilling God's mission.

What distinguishes the sense of call of those being appointed to overseas service from others? They have interpreted the call God extends to all of us as His people as a personal call. They recognize it as a purposeful call, a providential call, and an empowered call. This is reflected in the call of Moses at the burning-bush encounter with God in the book of Exodus.

> Meanwhile Moses was shepherding the flock of his
> father-in-law Jethro, the priest of Midian. He led the
> flock to the far side of the wilderness and came to
> Horeb, the mountain of God. Then the Angel of the
> LORD appeared to him in a flame of fire within a bush.
> As Moses looked, he saw that the bush was on fire but
> was not consumed. So Moses thought: I must go over
> and look at this remarkable sight. Why isn't the bush
> burning up?

When the LORD saw that he had gone over to look, God called out to him from the bush, "Moses, Moses!"

"Here I am," he answered.

"Do not come closer," He said. "Take your sandals off your feet, for the place where you are standing is holy ground." Then He continued, "I am the God of your father, the God of Abraham, the God of Isaac, and the God of Jacob." Moses hid his face because he was afraid to look at God.

Then the LORD said, "I have observed the misery of My people in Egypt, and have heard them crying out because of their oppressors, and I know about their sufferings. I have come down to rescue them from the power of the Egyptians. . . . The Israelites' cry for help has come to Me, and I have also seen the way the Egyptians are oppressing them. Therefore, go. I am sending you to Pharaoh so that you may lead My people, the Israelites, out of Egypt." (Exod. 3:1–10)

THE CALL OF GOD IS A PERSONAL CALL

God said that He had seen the oppression of His people and their need for deliverance. He said, "I have come down to rescue them," but He said to Moses, "I am sending you"! He said, "You are the one I am calling. You are the one I am going to use to deliver them from Pharaoh." This is a beautiful analogy of what happened when Jesus Christ came to earth and died on the cross to deliver a world from sin. God said, "I have seen the hopelessness of a world lost in sin. I have seen the futility of mankind trying to live a righteous life. I have seen the bondage to sin and the eternal lostness that awaits humanity. I am going to come down and bear that burden and deliver you from the eternal penalty of sin."

God told Moses that He would deliver His people from bondage in Egypt, but He personally called Moses to be the one He would use. Those going as missionaries are being appointed because they have heard the call of God personally. Yes, every Christian is called to missions. It is not a matter of who is to go and who is permitted to stay at home; every child of God has the responsibility to find their place in God's mission. For some it will be going. For others it will be sending and mobilizing, but no one is exempt from our Great Commission task.

But for those being appointed to service overseas, it has been a personal call. You have shared the diverse ways God has spoken into your life and revealed it wasn't enough to pray and to give and to go on a few short-term mission trips. You came to the conviction God has a place for you. Obedience requires leaving your familiar surroundings and comfortable lifestyle such as Moses enjoyed in the Midian desert. God has said, "You are the one I have chosen to deliver an unreached people group in South Asia from bondage to sin and darkness." He has said, "I am breaking resistance to the gospel in the Muslim world, and you are the one I am sending to proclaim the name of Jesus as the hope of salvation and deliverance." He has said, "I have come down and stirred global events to open a door of opportunity in the former communist world; I'm accelerating the harvest in China and the former Soviet Union, and you are the one I'm calling to reap that harvest." You have heard God's call, like Moses, as a personal call.

THE CALL OF GOD IS A PROVIDENTIAL CALL

That call is also a call from God Himself. It is not just a whim or emotional impression that has brought you to this point. You are not leaving your comfort zone and the security of family and friends to take your family to remote and dangerous places throughout the world because you are enamored by the opportunity of travel. You are certainly not going to serve as a missionary because of visions of financial gain and affluence.

Your family may not understand why you would do what you are doing, but there is only one explanation—God called you, and you have to be obedient. God made clear to Moses that the One speaking to Him was the God of Abraham, Isaac, and Jacob. Later when Moses asked for confirmation of who He was, somewhat indignantly God replied, "I am who I am." It is the One who is, the eternal Creator and Lord of the universe who was, who is, and forever will be. That is who is sending you to set His people free.

The word *providence* comes from two Latin words—*video* which means to see, and *pro* which means beforehand. God knows everything that is going to happen. He already knew that His people would be set free from bondage in Egypt. He knew how the confrontation with Pharaoh would go and how instrumental Moses would be in what God was going to do. And God knows exactly how He is going to use each of you. Because your call is from God and is a providential call, you can be assured that He is going to deliver your nation, city, or people group from bondage in sin. He has already mapped out the strategy to extend His kingdom into the lost dominions of the field where you will be assigned. Moses had no clue what all God was going to do through Him, just as you have no idea how your witness and ministry will unfold. Just like Moses, it won't be without opposition. It won't be without personal doubts. It won't be without discouragement and disappointments. But recognize that your call is a providential call from God Himself, and your response is not so much a decision to become a missionary as much as it is a commitment to the lordship of Jesus Christ, to follow in submission to His will and allow Him to use you as He chooses.

THE CALL OF GOD IS A PURPOSEFUL CALL

God made clear that He was calling Moses for the purpose of delivering His people from bondage. Recognize that your call is also for that same explicit purpose. You are going to the field to fill various assignments. Some of you are going as strategic coordinators, others as teachers and trainers. Some will be going to mission support as a counselor, business manager, bookkeeper, volunteer coordinator, or some other role. Some of you will be engaged in humanitarian relief projects, medical ministry, or to develop media tools. But the purpose for which you are going overseas is because a lost world needs to know Jesus. You could serve the Lord and do what you are going to do here in the United States, but God has seen the lostness, the oppression, and the suffering of those without Christ, and He is sending you to deliver them by sharing the good news of Jesus Christ.

Never lose sight of the purpose for which God has called you. Don't be diverted to other activities and ministries and lose the priority of evangelism. Don't allow the busyness and demands of survival in a cross-cultural setting to distract you from constantly seeing the lostness around you and being reminded that's why you are there—to deliver them from sin.

THE CALL OF GOD IS AN EMPOWERED CALL

God has not called you to go out on your own, dependent on your own resources. He said to Moses, "I will certainly be with you, and this will be the sign to you that I have sent you" (Exod. 3:12). God promises to go with you and empower you. His strength will empower you; His grace will sustain you. You do not fulfill God's call in your own ability. Most of you have been to seminary; you have had years of experience and training, but God did not call you because of your education and ability. You will be subjected to an extended time of orientation and training, but that is not what will make you effective for communicating the gospel in the context of cross-cultural worldviews.

The indwelling presence of God goes with you and equips you for the task. He has told us to be His witness to the ends of the earth, not because of our capabilities, but because it is predicated on having received the power of the Holy Spirit. The Great Commission is preceded by Jesus' claim that all power in heaven and earth had been given to Him, and it closes with the assurance that He will go with you as you go to make disciples of the nations.

Do you remember Moses' reaction to God's call? He began to make excuses. Just like some of you, he replied, "Who, me? Lord, the people won't listen and respond to me. Lord, I can't speak eloquently or fluently." You are probably thinking, *How will I ever learn a foreign language and be able to communicate in Chinese, Urdu, or Swahili; I can't even speak English very well!* Finally, Moses pleaded, "Let someone else go; call someone else." In response, we read in Exodus 4:14 that the anger of the Lord burned against Moses.

When God calls, you don't make excuses. It is not about your language competence, your leadership skills or lack thereof, because it is not about your ability. Because God called you, He will empower you. You are simply His instrument. God is intervening through global events to draw a lost world to Jesus Christ. But He has chosen you to go to the peoples of the world, to be the one through whom He has chosen to work. No one else can fulfill your call for you. It is a personal call, it is a providential call from God Himself, it is a purposeful call to deliver a lost world, and it is an empowered call.

29

Praise Among the Nations

Psalm 67

Many being appointed as missionaries think the reason they are going overseas is to save a lost world from sin. The motivation that brings them to the point of committing their life to serve God overseas is the awareness of the lostness of a world without Jesus Christ. Perhaps on a mission trip or short-term assignment with the IMB, they were confronted with people, indeed entire cultures, that were irreligious, following a futile path of empty ritual or striving for salvation through their own efforts and piety. One's heart cannot avoid being burdened by the need of someone to go and live among such people in order to share the hope that can be found in Jesus alone. But it was not just a burdened heart; those of you being appointed have said, "Here I am. Send me" (Isa. 6:8).

Some may have recognized the massive lostness of our world as they were daily confronted with news headlines of war, political upheaval, ethnic violence, and suffering. You read of masses dying in natural disasters and entering a Christless eternity because they had yet to be touched by a Christian witness. God stirred your heart to realize that you could not make Him Lord of your life and hold on to your own plans and isolate your serving Him in the provincialism of stateside comforts and security. If a world is to know Christ, you realized the Great Commission had to become personal and you had to be willing to be obedient to His call.

Whether the result of a short-term mission experience, a call to obedience to the lordship of Christ, or the realization since childhood that this is the plan and purpose that God had for your life, you are being sent out to proclaim the good news of the gospel to a lost world. Many of you are going where that message has already been made known. You are joining missionary colleagues and national church partners to push back the fringes of lostness in a growing harvest.

Others of you are going to pioneer assignments, breaking new ground, and through creative access platforms taking the gospel to unreached people groups that will hear it for the first time. You are going as doctors and nurses to engage in medical work. Others will use teaching roles or humanitarian ministries to gain acceptance among a population group that would not otherwise welcome a missionary witness. Some are going to fill more traditional roles as strategy coordinators, church planters, disciplers, and trainers, but the primary reason all of you are going is to share the gospel and win a lost world to saving faith in Jesus Christ.

But there is another reason God has called you to the nations. It is why you are compelled to give your lives to the people of India, Mozambique, Uganda, Indonesia, and places we cannot identify publicly in Northern Africa and East Asia. It is not just to populate heaven with people who are saved from hell, but the fact is that their salvation brings glory to God. He desires the praises of the nations and all the peoples of the world to experience the joy of being born again.

Psalm 67:1–4 says, "May God be gracious to us and bless us; look on us with favor so that Your way may be known on earth, Your salvation among all nations. Let the peoples praise You, God; let all the peoples praise You. Let the nations rejoice and shout for joy."

GOD WANTS THE PEOPLES OF THE EARTH TO KNOW HIM

God had called Israel as His special, chosen people, not just to bless them, to bring them to the promised land and prosper their every endeavor. They were to be a missions people, an instrument to fulfill His mission to make His way known in the earth, and to declare His salvation among all nations. God wanted everyone to know of His salvation.

During our year of language study upon arrival in Indonesia, I was attempting to translate sermon notes into Indonesian. In this sermon I had used the term "redemptive love." My Muslim language tutor affirmed I had correctly translated the words, but he did not comprehend the concept. When I explained the love of God that redeemed us from sin and provided salvation, his response was to say, "We don't have anything like that in our religion."

God said in Isaiah 45:22, "Turn to Me and be saved, all the ends of the earth. For I am God, and there is no other." God wants all the world to know that He is their salvation, that Jesus Christ is Savior. As the apostles declared, "There is salvation in no one else, for there is no other name under heaven given to people by which we must be saved" (Acts. 4:12).

Not only does God want the nations to know that He is Savior; He wants them to know that He is sovereign over all the earth. The psalmist goes on in verse 4 to say, "You judge the peoples with fairness and lead the nations on earth" (Ps. 67:4). God is the one conducting the affairs of nations. His providence takes human events and conforms them to His purpose. Isaiah 14:24 declares, "The

LORD of Hosts has sworn: As I have planned, so it will be; as I have purposed it, so it will happen." Psalm 47:7–8 reminds us what God wants the world to know, "For God is King of all the earth. God reigns over the nations; God is seated on His holy throne."

God wants the peoples of the earth to know that He is Savior, that He is sovereign, and also that He is the source of all blessings. The psalmist puts this in perspective: "The earth has produced its harvest; God, our God, blesses us" (Ps. 67:6). He wants the nations to know that they do not receive the produce of their crops and economic growth by their own efforts and ingenuity. God is the one who installs the cycle of the seasons and gives the rain and sun. God's blessing allows developing nations to prosper. But it is for the purpose that they would recognize it is from Him. God desires all the peoples would praise Him with joy and gladness as recipients of His salvation, in recognition of His sovereignty and as the source of all blessings.

Recently, my wife and I traveled to Vietnam and Cambodia. It was amazing to see the development and progress that had been made in these Third-World countries since our last visit about ten years ago. With a massive labor force and aid from abroad, Vietnam has emerged as a major economic power in Southeast Asia. The occasion of our trip was to attend the first open, government-sanctioned convention of Baptists in that country. Baptists, representing more than three hundred house churches that have emerged, gathered publicly and were recognized by government officials. Leaders of the country have learned that religious freedom is expected by those attaining acceptance in international relations and trade. They haven't come to realize that God has had something to do with their economic progress, but His name is being praised in that country as never before.

WHY GOD WANTS THE PEOPLES OF THE EARTH TO KNOW HIM

God wants them to know Him, His way, and salvation because of the tragedy of lostness. We are grateful that we live in America where churches can worship freely. We are privileged to have been born and to live in a place where the gospel can be shared openly. We praise God because one day someone told us about Jesus, and as we responded in faith, we knew with full assurance that our sins were forgiven and that our eternal destiny is in heaven. It is hard for us to comprehend the tragedy of lostness throughout the world. We know someone in our neighborhood or family who has not trusted Jesus is lost and bound for hell, but can we grasp the scope of billions living and dying outside God's grace?

Over one billion Muslims devoutly pray to Allah and affirm Mohammed as his prophet, but their prayers are directed to a concept of a distant, impersonal deity that cannot be known; the possibility of heaven is a fatalistic hope that can never be assured. Multitudes of Buddhists have no concept of a personal God and strive in futility for an unknown eternal destiny through their own good works. Many of these have heard of Jesus but choose to follow the influence and path of their cultural traditions. Even more tragic are the 1.3 billion people among unreached people groups who have never heard the name of Jesus. There is no church in their midst to bear a Christian witness, no Scripture in their language by which they might read of the way, the truth, and the life, and no Christian neighbor through whom they might be drawn to know God.

But the greatest tragedy is not just the lostness of multitudes of people or even their lack of opportunity to hear and respond to the gospel. The greatest tragedy is that He alone who is worthy of all honor and praise and power and glory—Almighty God—is being deprived of the praises of those He created, loves, and died to save.

I remember Dr. Tom Elliff telling me about a mission trip he and several members from his former church took to Cambodia. One afternoon a missionary took them to a Buddhist monastery where he had been teaching English to the monks. Although feeling somewhat awkward in that setting, the group from Oklahoma found the monks gracious and hospitable, delighted to meet friends from America and to have the opportunity to practice their English. Tom related that they were receptive as the group shared their Christian testimony and, although unplanned, sang some Christian worship choruses for their hosts. Spontaneously, Tom suggested that these Buddhist monks sing some of their songs for the group. They started a dissonant Buddhist chant and, apparently realizing how it sounded, one of them said, "We don't have any songs in our religion."

Did you realize that Christians are the only ones who sing? Millions of Buddhists and Hindus throughout Asia know nothing of God's redemptive grace that would elicit a song of praise in their hearts. Millions of Muslims who do not know of a loving God who longs to save them have nothing for which to express their joy in songs of loving praise and adoration. Multitudes of people groups still in bondage to spiritual darkness, hopelessness, and despair are not singing praise to the God who is the Savior, Sovereign, and Source of all blessing.

The nations are not glad and singing for joy, and God is deprived of the praises of the people. Most of the world does not even know why they were born upon the earth—that it was so they would one day join that heavenly choir around the throne of God. When we sing the hymn "O for a Thousand Tongues to Sing," we are not singing about a record attendance on Sunday morning; we are singing about thousands of languages from every tribe and people joining in a mighty chorus giving praise to the One who sits upon the throne and to the Lamb who was worthy to be slain.

How Are All the Peoples of the Earth Going to Know and Praise God?

Psalm 67 tells us in the first and last verses: "May God be gracious to us and bless us; look on us with favor. . . . God will bless us, and all the ends of the earth will fear Him." Israel realized that God had been gracious and blessed them, not for their own benefit, but so that His way would be known throughout the earth and all the nations would praise Him. They were to be a people to fulfill His mission.

To those being appointed as missionaries, God has been gracious to you and blessed you. He saved you out of a life of sin, turned your life around, and has faithfully led you to this point of giving your life to serve Him on the mission field. It is not because you are worthy. It is not because of your education and abilities but because of His grace. Some may feel sorry for you that you are having to leave your family and loved ones to live in a dangerous and remote location on the other side of the world. But no, you are the privileged ones. God has blessed you. His face shines upon you for you are the ones God has chosen to make His way known upon the earth that all peoples and nations would be glad and sing His praise!

30

Maintaining Focus

Luke 4:42–5:11

Many people have the impression that the Great Commission was an afterthought to the teachings of Jesus. Having completed His earthly ministry and ready to ascend to the Father, He gathered with His disciples on a mountain in Galilee for a final word of exhortation when it occurred to Him, "Oh, by the way, why don't you go and make disciples of other nations." The Great Commission wasn't an afterthought; it began in the heart of God from the foundation of the world. And it was reflected in the life and teaching of Jesus from the earliest days of His ministry.

Chapter 4 of the Gospel of Luke records the first day of Jesus' ministry. In the earlier chapters we have an extended account of His birth and boyhood as well as the account of His baptism and temptation experience in the wilderness. His ministry began at the synagogue in Nazareth where He read from Isaiah 61 and revealed that His coming was the fulfillment of this Messianic prophecy. He was rejected by those in His hometown, and that afternoon He went down to Capernaum where He healed Simon's mother-in-law.

As the sun set on that first Sabbath Day, we are told that the whole city came to see Him as He healed the sick, cast out demons, and proclaimed the kingdom of God.

It should be noted that here at the beginning of Jesus' ministry, (1) He determined the priority of His purpose, (2) He demonstrated the power of His presence, and (3) He demanded participation in His program.

Those of you being appointed as missionaries are getting ready to begin your ministry overseas. Many of you have been on volunteer trips or served in short-term assignments on the mission field. You may already know something of the challenges you will face as you seek to share the gospel cross-culturally. You will be overwhelmed with the masses of people and the needs. As you take the gospel to places in Northern Africa, Burkina Faso, Italy, France, Brazil, and Peru, you will find many demands pulling you in multiple directions. You will be stretched as you learn the language, adapt to an austere lifestyle, and seek to provide for the needs of your family. It is important, like Jesus, at the beginning of your ministry, to identify your priorities, learn to depend upon the power of His presence, and know what it means to participate in God's plan and mission.

Jesus Determined the Priority of His Purpose

The next morning after the remarkable response of the crowds in Capernaum, Jesus arose early to pray and spend time with the Father. This became a pattern of His life because it was important for Him to stay in touch with the will and purpose God had set for Him. The disciples were looking for Him, and the people came, trying to keep Him from going away. But He said in reply, "I must proclaim the good news about the kingdom of God to the other towns also, because I was sent for this purpose" (Luke 4:43).

Jesus determined the priority of His purpose. It wasn't just to preach the gospel in His hometown. It wasn't just to proclaim the kingdom where people would respond. His purpose was to preach the kingdom of God in every city; His priority was to give all people an opportunity to hear and respond to the gospel. Never forget that the priority of your purpose, wherever God is sending you, is to give everyone an opportunity to hear and respond to the gospel. You may be going as a teacher, an accountant, or a business manager. You may be assigned to do media work, medical ministry, or engage in humanitarian projects, but your job assignment is not your priority. God is placing you where you are going because people are lost and need to hear the gospel. The priority of your purpose is to bear witness to the saving power of the gospel, tell them a Savior has come, and proclaim Jesus Christ to everyone.

Missionaries tend to find a niche of ministry and devote themselves to a handful of people who have been receptive and with whom they have built a relationship. That's good; nurturing a small group to faith is how churches are started. But don't become so focused on a responsive group that you neglect, in your busyness and scheduled activities, the multitudes around you who are ignored. Many personnel going to restricted countries on creative access platforms tend to substitute presence for proclamation. We are intrigued to gained entry to a place where traditional missionaries are not allowed, as if one's mere presence will bring people to Christ. He has sent you with a message that must be communicated and made known, sometimes discretely, but never forget that is the priority of your purpose and why you go as a missionary.

A group of church planters, with whom we worked years ago in Indonesia, identified a principle that responsiveness was directly proportional to the distance from the main highway. The most remote villages were where we found the greatest response. As I would nurture people in those locations to become a church,

I realized I passed towns and villages with multitudes of people along the way. Did they not deserve to hear the gospel? How could I justify neglecting them in my witness and efforts at church planting? Jesus would say to you, and all of us, the priority of God's purpose—and our calling—is to preach the gospel of the kingdom to every city, every nation, and every people group.

JESUS DEMONSTRATED THE POWER OF HIS PRESENCE

As we move into chapter 5 of Luke's Gospel, we find Jesus standing in a boat a little ways offshore teaching the people the next morning. The disciples had returned to the lake fishing during the night; this was the occasion when they fished all night and didn't catch anything. What happened as Jesus finished His sermon is significant: "When He had finished speaking, He said to Simon, 'Put out into deep water and let down your nets for a catch.' 'Master,' Simon replied, 'we've worked hard all night long and caught nothing! But at Your word, I'll let down the nets.' When they did this, they caught a great number of fish, and their nets began to tear" (Luke 5:4–6).

What made the difference? The disciples were experienced fishermen who knew how to catch fish on the Sea of Galilee, but they had not been successful. What made the difference? It was the presence of Jesus. Wherever Jesus goes, He manifests the power of His presence by drawing in the net, the harvest of souls.

Never think for a moment that in all your education and the training you will receive before you go to the field, that you have the ability to convince anyone of the truth of Christianity. You can study apologetics; you can learn about the cultural worldviews of Muslims, Hindus, animists, or postmodern secularists, but you don't have the power to save anyone. It is the work of the Holy Spirit to convict them of sin and the truth of the gospel. As you proclaim and lift up Jesus Christ, His power will soften their hearts and draw them to faith. Why would Jesus tell us to be witnesses, even to the ends of the earth, in Acts 1:8? It is because that expectation is predicated on the fact we receive the power of the Holy Spirit.

Before Jesus gave the Great Commission and commanded us to go and make disciples of all nations, He said, "All authority has been given to Me in heaven and on earth" (Matt. 28:18). Missionaries are sent in obedience to this Great Commission challenge, not because of their ability and qualifications. As you go to reach the nations, the indwelling presence of Jesus Christ goes with you. You go in His power and authority.

All over the world Jesus is demonstrating the power of His presence in drawing people to salvation. As we saw in our earlier report, last year alone almost 610,000 new believers were baptized, many of these among unreached people groups that are hearing the gospel for the first time. I had the privilege of going to such a group last month in visiting our Extreme Team in the jungles of the Amazon Basin in Peru. After a flight to a city in the northwestern part of the country, we flew in a chartered flight to a remote landing strip near the border with Brazil. After a five-hour ride in a motorized dugout canoe, we reached a Yaminahua village where three Journeymen had been living a couple of years. There is now a thriving church among these indigenous tribal people because Jesus demonstrated the power of His presence in the lives of these young missionaries and in the gospel message they proclaimed.

JESUS DEMANDED PARTICIPATION IN HIS PROGRAM

Finally, we should note that Jesus demanded participation in His program. Immediately after the great catch of fish, He said to His disciples and those around Him, "Don't be afraid. . . . From now on you will be catching people!" (Luke 5:10). Jesus has a program and a plan to proclaim the gospel to all the people, cities, and nations.

His program is to extend the kingdom of God to all peoples, and we are the ones He calls to carry out that program. It is a call to follow Him. It is a call to become His disciples, equipped to become like Him in character and ministry, and then to become fishers of men. We are to intentionally go after a lost world, proclaiming the gospel, bearing witness in the power of God's Spirit and drawing others into the kingdom. That is not just a demand on those who go as missionaries but for everyone who will be a follower of Jesus.

Notice the response of the disciples: "Then they brought the boats to land, left everything, and followed Him" (Luke 5:11). Many are looking at those of you going as missionaries and thinking that is exactly what you have done. You have left a prominent church ministry to go overseas. You have walked away from a successful business or professional career in obedience to God's call. You have sold your nice, comfortable American dream home and are facing extended separation from family and loved ones, and you probably think you are leaving everything to become a missionary.

But I want to alert you that this is a decision you will need to make continually. When you get to the mission field, a sense of entitlement begins to emerge. You begin to justify focusing on things that make life comfortable and convenient; you want a comfortable house and find yourself spending an inordinate amount of time providing for the needs of your family. It is a continuing challenge to forsake all for the cause of Christ. It is a continual call to lay your life on the altar that God might entrust you with His power and use you as fishers of men for His glory.

You will have no greater thrill than telling someone about Jesus who has never heard. You will have no greater blessing than the privilege of seeing the kingdom of God planted among a people or in a community where no Christian witness has ever previously existed. God has determined the priority of His purpose, He has demonstrated the power of His presence, and He is calling you to participate in His program.

31

The Power of Your Witness

1 Thessalonians 1:5–9

This is truly an auspicious time to be appointed to missionary service. Those of you going to the ends of the earth have to be aware of the formidable challenges you are facing. The headlines scream with daily reports of violence, warfare, ethnic conflicts, political disruption, and lately, an economic meltdown that is sweeping the globe. You will find increasing hostility all over the world, not only because of your Christian witness, but because you are an American. In fact, most of you are going to places that do not welcome missionaries, and you cannot even identify the specific location of your assignment publicly.

Yet you are going out at a time of unprecedented harvest and response to the gospel. Through creative access strategies you are using your skills and experience in secular vocations, to go to places that value what you have to offer. As you plant your life among lost cultures and people groups, you have the unique opportunity to build relationships, communicate the love of Christ, and plant the gospel in places where people are longing for the hope and assurance that only Jesus can provide.

EXAMPLES OF A POWERFUL, MULTIPLYING WITNESS

Earlier this year I had the privilege to go to Southeast Asia, primarily to attend the first open, government-sanctioned convention of Baptists in Vietnam. For years, Christians have labored under repressive communist restrictions, but as the country emerges in a prominent role of international commerce, they are recognizing that human rights and religious freedom are expected. I was thrilled to discover that over the years the gospel had continued to spread through the faithful witness of believers who were undeterred by threats and restrictions, and more than three hundred churches had been planted.

Visiting Cambodia, I recalled when our first personnel went into the killing fields of that country, decimated by the Khmer Rouge. The country was still under a communist government, and an open Christian witness was prohibited. But the country was destitute, in need of social ministries and rehabilitation. We had some personnel with those skills who were willing to risk going into that repressive situation. Two years later they reported twenty-four house churches had emerged in the capital city of Phnom Penh. After another two years, a Baptist convention was organized with forty churches throughout the country, and today, 260 churches continue to spread the gospel.

My last overseas trip was across the 10/40 Window of Northern Africa, the Arabian Peninsula, the Horn of Africa, and Turkey—gateway to the Persian and Turkic world of Central Asia. In this Muslim heart of darkness, we found believers and church groups multiplying. One university student who had dared to confess his faith openly told us many of the students are reading the Bible, searching for spiritual truth because they are disillusioned with what they see reflected in the terrorist activity and repressive nature of their traditional faith. In China, some researchers are reporting as many as thirty thousand believers a day coming to faith in Christ. One of our church planters envisioned being a part of a movement to see two hundred house churches started during his four-year term there but saw that number surpassed after only six months. In another country where a church-planting movement is taking place, I asked one of our missionaries how this was happening. In a classic understatement he replied, "The poor don't get much good news."

The power of the gospel brings hope to spiritually destitute hearts. I could not count the number of missionaries who have shared testimonies of penetrating an unreached people group or accessing a village that had never heard the gospel and finding people receptive; the people say, "We have been waiting all our lives for someone to bring us this message." There is no explanation for the spread of the gospel except for the power of God that indwells that message. It makes no sense for a Muslim student to turn his back on his culture, religion, and society and embrace faith in Jesus Christ knowing he will be ostracized, disowned by his family, and even his life will be threatened. It is evidence of the power of God's love and the story of salvation that resonates within the heart of those who are lost, living in despair, under the burden of sin, and without hope.

Each missionary is appointed to fill a specific assignment, but the purpose for going overseas is to plant your life among people who are lost to tell them about Jesus. Paul's testimony in 1 Thessalonians describes the nature of your witness and what God desires to do through you. Paul is reflecting on the gospel coming to the people of Thessalonica, and he says,

> For our gospel did not come to you in word only,
> but also in power, in the Holy Spirit, and with much
> assurance. You know what kind of men we were among

you for your benefit, and you became imitators of us
and of the Lord when, in spite of severe persecution,
you welcomed the message with the joy from the Holy
Spirit. As a result, you became an example to all the
believers in Macedonia and Achaia. For the Lord's
message rang out from you, not only in Macedonia and
Achaia, but in every place that your faith in God has
gone out, so we don't need to say anything. For they
themselves report about us what kind of reception we
had from you: how you turned to God from idols to
serve the living and true God. (1 Thess. 1:5–9)

Don't miss the significance of what is happening. The people
in Thessalonica received the gospel, and they spontaneously shared
their faith throughout the city and the province. As other believers
accepted the gospel, their witness spread into the neighboring
provinces of Macedonia and Achaia and beyond. As Paul continued
his itinerant preaching throughout the area, he found that everywhere
he went he did not have to tell them about Jesus; they had already
heard. And not only had they heard; they had also seen the evidence
of the transforming power of the gospel in the lives of those who had
turned from idols to serve the living and true God.

Isn't that what you want to see happen in the place where you
are going? Wouldn't you like to see your witness multiply through
those you win to Christ and disciple? Most of you are going to places
of massive population. You will never personally be able to witness
to everyone. But note the nature of the gospel. Once it is received
and one's life is transformed, it cannot be restrained regardless of
government restrictions, religious opposition, and personal threats
or persecution. Last year missionaries reported more than twenty-
five thousand new churches started; over 600,000 new believers were
baptized. That is not the result of IMB strategy or clever church-
planting methodology. It is the result of the same thing that was

happening in Thessalonica in the book of Acts and throughout the New Testament.

CHARACTERISTICS OF A POWERFUL, MULTIPLYING WITNESS

First, it must be an intentional, empowered witness. These believers in Thessalonica did not receive the gospel in word only but in power, the Holy Spirit, and full conviction. They did not just embrace teaching about a new religion; it was a relevant, life-changing experience that they were compelled to share with others. Among a South Asian people group where believers have been martyred for their faith, new converts reflect that conviction as they are taught a litany in case they are arrested and their life threatened. They say, "You do not take my life from me, but I gladly give my life for my Lord Jesus Christ that one day you, too, may know Him."

One of our personnel was teaching a group of house church pastors on baptism. He said that they must ask the candidate three questions: "Do you believe that Jesus Christ is the Son of God who died for the sins of the world? Are you receiving Jesus as your personal Savior? Are you making a commitment to live for Him as Lord of your life?" If they answer "yes" to all three, then you may baptize them. But the house church leaders responded with insistence a fourth question be asked before they are eligible for baptism: "If the authorities drag you out of your home, arrest you, threaten your family, and take all your belongings, will you still follow Jesus?"

When you have that kind of conviction, your witness has power that cannot be inhibited or deterred. People observe that the Christian faith is not just a way of life but something worth dying for. The world is looking for something beyond empty ritual and religious tradition; they are looking for the assurance of a relevant, authentic, life-transforming experience.

Second, it must be an incarnational witness. How did the
believers in Thessalonica become this kind of witness? That was
what they observed in Paul and his companions. Paul said, "You
know what kind of men we were among you for your benefit, and
you became imitators of us and of the Lord" (1 Thess. 1:5–6).
They were simply imitating the example of Paul's life and witness,
doing what he did, and that example continued to spread. We have
discovered the effectiveness of this in our T4T training—training for
trainers around the world. When someone is led to faith in Christ,
they are taught and challenged to immediately share that experience
with ten others among their friends and family. Why wait for months
of discipleship training or years of growth to maturity to become
a witness for Christ? Then as a new convert is led through basic
discipleship, it is taught in a way that he can teach it to others.

The most effective witness is an incarnational witness—the
example of your life being lived out before a lost world. You are being
appointed as missionaries because Jesus told us to go. When a lost
world sees the reality of Christ in your life, it earns you credibility
for presenting a verbal witness. Wouldn't it be wonderful if you could
say, like Paul, to those you win and disciple, "Just watch my life. Live
like I live; do what I do, and the result will be Christlikeness. You
will become imitators not just of me but of the Lord!"

Third, it must be an infinitely infectious witness. One
of the most powerful aspects of their witness was that "in spite of
severe persecution," they "welcomed the message with the joy from
the Holy Spirit" (1 Thess. 1:6). The world to which you are going
doesn't have much joy. In fact, it is a world filled with suffering and
despair—refugees in a war-torn environment and multitudes living
in darkness without hope among unreached people groups. The joy
of salvation that Jesus brings is infectious. It even supersedes the
suffering, adversity, and tribulation in this world. Now, you better

believe that gets people's attention! It becomes something that draws them to Jesus.

Don't ever presume that God is going to put a hedge of protection around you and keep you from trials and hardship because you are committed to serve Him. To the contrary, He knows that your most effective witness may be the victorious faith you exhibit when you experience an accident or illness or lose your belongings in looting and violence. When people see you receive news of the loss of a loved one and see your faith remain steadfast, they will clamor to know what makes the difference and embrace the faith to which you witness.

QUALIFICATIONS FOR A POWERFUL, MULTIPLYING WITNESS

Intimacy with God. If people are to see a faith that is more than words, but see conviction, power, and the Holy Spirit in your life, then you must have a personal intimacy with God. This comes only from spending time with Him on your knees in humble submission, acknowledging your desperate need for His grace and power. It comes from immersing yourself in His Word, which builds faith and boldness. It means practicing the presence of Jesus so that people do not see you but Christ in you.

Immersion with the people. If you are to have a powerful witness that multiplies, you must spend time with people. Too often we have a "popcorn" witness. We meet with a group once a week— we pop in, pop off, and pop out, and they don't see us until the next week when we pop in, pop off, and pop out again. Where was Paul day in and day out? He was in the marketplace, making tents, interacting with the people. They observed his lifestyle and attitude and imitated his faith.

Identification with suffering. Finally, as James 1:2 says, "Consider it a great joy . . . whenever you experience various trials."

Don't feel forsaken when adversity comes. It may be your greatest opportunity for people to see the reality of a victorious, living Savior in your life. It is that kind of powerful witness that will multiply spontaneously.

32

Praying for God's Provision

Colossians 1:3–11

As you go to the mission field, you will be surrounded by a "great cloud of witnesses." They include family and friends and many others whom you do not know personally. They represent a vast multitude of Southern Baptists who undergird your ministry with their support and prayers. While the International Mission Board channels the financial support and benefits that enable you to fulfill your call to overseas service, we would be remiss to allow you to go to the field without the assurance of prayer support. You are entering Satan's territory and will engage in spiritual warfare. You will be challenged by cross-cultural adjustments and language learning. You will be confronted with your own inadequacy and become desperate for resources only God can provide. That's why you are required to enlist those who will partner with you and pray every day for you.

The apostle Paul encountered the same challenges, and his epistles are saturated with prayers and requests for prayer. His prayer for the believers in Colossae could reflect our prayer for you as you prepare to go to the mission field. In Colossians 1:3–5 he writes,

"We always thank God, the Father of our Lord Jesus Christ, when we pray for you, for we have heard of your faith in Christ Jesus and of the love which you have for all saints because of the hope reserved for you in heaven."

We are thankful for you. We praise God for His calling upon your life. We have heard your testimony of faith to go to a foreign field and trust God to care for you, and we believe you will see fruit from your labor. We thank God for the love He has placed in your hearts, not only for the saints, but also for a lost world. Only love makes possible the phenomena of sacrifice. Love is others-centered, and that is the only thing that would compel you to turn your back on the comforts and security of home and the potential success of an American lifestyle, to plant your life among those who need to know Jesus. And we praise God for the hope that you have in Him, not just for your own reward in heaven, but the hope of those from every language, people, and nation sharing that assured hope that can be found in Jesus Christ.

So I would hope those in your church and everyone who knows you will feel the responsibility—as Paul expressed it—to pray always for you. And we can do so with confidence because you are going out into a world in which God is at work. As Paul reflects, "The gospel that has come to you . . . is bearing fruit and growing" (Col. 1:6). That is because the gospel you proclaim is the power of God to draw people to Jesus Christ. God is using the warfare and violence throughout the world, political disruption, economic uncertainty, natural disasters, and suffering to turn the hearts of people to what only Jesus can provide. You, too, will need what only God can provide. Paul prayed for God's spiritual provisions for this New Testament church, and his prayer reflects exactly what you need as well. So we pray, like Paul, that (1) you will be filled with the knowledge of His will, (2) you will walk in a manner worthy of the Lord, and (3) you will be strengthened with all power.

FILLED WITH THE KNOWLEDGE OF GOD'S WILL

Paul's prayer continues: "We haven't stopped praying for you. We are asking that you may be filled with the knowledge of His will in all wisdom and spiritual understanding" (Col. 1:9). You would not be here tonight if you did not have a strong conviction of God's will leading you to the places you are going to serve. Some of you sense God's will leading you to Latin America, while God has revealed His will to others to go to Africa or Asia. God's will has been confirmed for some of you to join colleagues reaping the harvest, discipling believers, and planting churches where the gospel can be freely shared; but others of you have a conviction of God's will to plant your lives among unreached people groups. Perhaps you have struggled, like many, to know God's will and whether or not He was leading you to missionary service. But now in retrospect you are here tonight being sent out because you know this is God's will.

But this is only the beginning of a pilgrimage in which you are going to need discernment of His will. You will face many decisions about where to locate, how to identify a man of peace, and other strategic decisions. The answers will not be evident by logical reasoning and personal insights. You will need spiritual wisdom and understanding that come from God. In another epistle, Paul poses the rhetorical question, "Who can know the mind of God?" He proceeds to explain that only the Spirit can know the mind of God, and we have been given God's Spirit to reveal His will and direction. God's wisdom will reveal what you are to do, and understanding will enable you to know how to do it and why. So the knowledge of God's will is not just a one-time vocational decision but a daily experience of appropriating wisdom and understanding that comes from Him.

WALK IN A MANNER WORTHY OF THE LORD

Why did he pray for you to have this knowledge of God's will? It is evident as Paul continues his prayer: "So that you may walk worthy of the Lord, fully pleasing [to Him], bearing fruit in every good work and growing in the knowledge of God" (Col. 1:10). Keep in mind that your responsibility is not just to fulfill a job description. You are planting your life in an incarnational witness that is to reflect the reality of Jesus Christ within you. You are God's representative in a lost world. You may be restricted in being able to proclaim a verbal witness; it may be difficult to communicate biblical truths to those in a culture with a pagan worldview. Your most effective witness may be the life that you live that is different from anything they have ever seen before. They need to see abiding peace even in the midst of adversity. They need to see joy in every circumstance. They need to see a selfless love and grace as you give yourself to others rather than living for your own gain and benefit. Be sure the life you live is worthy of the Lord and is pleasing to Him.

A life worthy of the Lord and pleasing to Him will bear fruit in good works. Your assignment may not primarily entail humanitarian ministry to the poor and needy or counseling and encouraging the distressed, but a lifestyle and love and caring for others is expected of anyone who belongs to Jesus Christ and presumes to serve Him. First Peter 2:12 tells us, "Conduct yourselves honorably among the Gentiles, so that in a case where they speak against you as those who do evil, they may, by observing your good works, glorify God in a day of visitation." Those who would otherwise slander and reject the Christian message will change their attitude and embrace the gospel when they observe your good deeds among them.

That doesn't come from your own character and inclination; in fact, the crowds and heat will become an irritation that will make you want to withdraw in isolation. That's why Paul adds that a life worthy of the Lord is one increasing in the knowledge of God. We pray that will be your experience. You already know Him; in fact, you probably have an intimacy and walk with the Lord that exceeds most Christians, but when you get on the field, you will be confronted with your inadequacy as never before and the need to know Him in a deeper, more meaningful way. That is not an increasing knowledge about God but knowing Him in a personal, experiential way and the reality of His power and grace.

STRENGTHENED WITH ALL POWER

Remember that this prayer of Paul is included in God's inspired Word. That indicates it reflects what God desires for us. God's desire is for you to be filled with the knowledge of His will and that you walk in a manner worthy of the Lord. Finally, the climactic supplication for these believers, as it is for each of you, is that you might be "strengthened with all power, according to His glorious might." The object of this prayer request is "for all endurance and patience, with joy" (Col. 1:11).

You do not go to the mission field limited to your own strength and ability. Jesus preceded the Great Commission with the claim that all power had been given unto Him in heaven and earth. Then He closed by affirming that He goes with us even to the end of the age. You carry to the mission field the indwelling presence of Jesus Christ Himself with all His power and authority. But you must appropriate that power by faith, believing and claiming all that has been made available to you. You forfeit the power of God when you try to do it yourself and resort to your own ability. Recognize every day, even every moment, that you are helpless and need His power, then yield in humble submission to His lordship.

Interestingly, Paul prays that these believers would be strengthened with all power, not just so their witness would be effective and bear fruit in an evangelistic harvest; it was so that they would be steadfast and patient. He was praying out of personal experience. He had been there. He knew how difficult it was to wait upon the Lord. He knew our tendency to anxiety and discouragement when things don't go as we expected and we don't always see the fruit of our labors. You will need not just an empowered witness but the power and strength to persevere, remain steadfast and patient to see the results in God's timing.

We are a generation that wants to see results. The world has convinced us we are entitled to fulfillment and success; if we don't see it, it is time to move on to greener pastures and look for other opportunities. But taking the kingdom of God to the nations requires patience and perseverance upheld by a vision that may extend even beyond our lifetime. When I began to work in a leadership role throughout South and Southeast Asia, I was impressed to find many veteran missionaries who had labored faithfully for thirty and forty years just to see a small congregation planted in a place extremely resistant to the gospel.

You also need His strength in order to joyously give thanks to the Father. The Bible instructs us to give thanks in all things. I learned early in our tenure on the field that this was a key to practicing the presence of Jesus and remaining mindful of the power and victory He provides. In times of disappointment and adversity, when plans go awry or even when we experience personal tragedy, praising God takes our focus off the circumstances and puts them on Him. When our thoughts are on God, we are mindful of His presence, and He is able to take control of our emotions, feelings, and attitudes and restore the joy and sense of victory.

So we pray for God's provision as we send you out that you will be filled with the knowledge of God's will, that you will walk in a manner worthy of the Lord, and that you will be strengthened with all power according to His glorious might!

33

The Reluctant Missionary

Jonah 1–4

Jonah is a missionary with whom many of you can identify. The unique story of being swallowed by a whale overshadows a more prominent message of a rejected missionary call, a second chance, and a marvelous reflection of God's compassion and mercy. The story of Jonah, as much as any biblical narrative, is often met with cynicism and ridicule. One commentary noted that many a skeptic will have to recant when they meet Jonah in heaven still covered in seaweed, blanched white by the stomach enzymes of that great fish! But the message of this brief Old Testament book is relevant today and a challenge to you who go in responsive obedience to God's call. It is a message of a concern revealed, a call resisted, and a compassion rewarded.

A CONCERN REVEALED

The account begins in the first two verses of chapter 1, with God's call. "The word of the LORD came to Jonah son of Amittai: 'Get up!

Go to the great city of Nineveh and preach against it, because their wickedness has confronted Me'" (Jon. 1:1–2). Following Jonah's deliverance, God gave him a second chance. Just as He continued to pursue many of you with His call to missions, we read in chapter 3, "Then the word of the Lᴏʀᴅ came to Jonah a second time: 'Get up! Go to the great city of Nineveh and preach the message that I tell you.' So Jonah got up and went to Nineveh according to the Lᴏʀᴅ's command" (Jon. 3:1–3).

It appears that God had lost His patience and was fed up with the wickedness of Nineveh, and He sent Jonah to proclaim a message of judgment. But did not God know that they would repent when convicted of their sin and pending judgment? God did not need anyone to tell them of the consequences of their sin and wickedness; He could have just wiped them out and been done with it. No, He knew that once they were confronted with the certainty of judgment, they would repent and turn to the Lord. Otherwise, why would He have been so persistent in sending a messenger to declare the word of the Lord?

God doesn't delight in the condemnation of a lost world. Many individuals reject the offer of salvation and grace, spurn the wooing of God's Holy Spirit and turn their backs on Jesus. But, confronted with the conviction of their sin and prospects of judgment by a holy and righteous God, and facing an eternity separated from Him in hell, they repent and come to Jesus in saving faith. Anyone who has never received Jesus Christ as personal Lord and Savior faces the same consequences as Nineveh. You may not characterize yourself as a wicked person; in fact, you may live a moral life and even attend church. God yearns to show compassion and forgive your sins and restore you to eternal fellowship with Him if you will believe on the One who gave His life and died for your sins that you might be saved.

God's concern for Nineveh is the same concern that He has for the cities and peoples of the world today that are facing His judgment because they do not know of His certain wrath on all who have never heard the good news of salvation and had the opportunity to believe on Jesus Christ. In a meeting last week with overseas missionary team leaders, we heard of 180 cities in China alone with more than a million people. More than half have not been evangelized in spite of a growing house-church movement that is spreading throughout the country. Having lived in some of the large metropolises of America, you can appreciate the challenge of evangelizing a massive city, but it is difficult to comprehend cities as massive as Tokyo, Sao Paulo, Brazil, and Mexico City, each with almost twenty million people. Researchers tell us half the world is now urbanized. Cairo, Istanbul, Bangkok, Moscow, and Jakarta are the Ninevehs of today, lost and facing eternal destruction unless someone is willing to go and warn them and reveal the available mercy of God.

God puts that impetus on us. In Ezekiel 3:18 we are told, "If I say to the wicked person: You will surely die, but you do not warn him—you don't speak out to warn him about his wicked way in order to save his life—that wicked person will die for his iniquity. Yet I will hold you responsible for his blood." Judgment and death are certain for the unrepentant, whether those in our own neighborhood in America who live in the shadow of a church, or those in far-off lands who have never heard the gospel. Jesus said, "Unless you repent, you will all perish as well" (Luke 13:3). We are told in Romans 10:13, "Everyone who calls on the name of the Lord will be saved." But then we are confronted with the question, "How can they call on Him in whom they have not believed? And how can they believe without hearing about Him? And how can they hear without a preacher?" (v. 14).

That is why God has called you to go overseas. That is why you are being appointed and being sent out to warn them and tell them of One in whom they can believe and be delivered from the inevitable judgment for sin. Like Jonah, you are not going to save them yourself or with your own message of admonition and advice. You are going to proclaim the word of the Lord that Jesus saves.

A CALL RESISTED

Jonah is often maligned for his disobedience and presuming to run from the call of God, but we have to admit that he is actually typical of a lot of Christians today. How many times did God have to call to get your attention and break through a resistant will? I have read the bio-data of those of you being appointed, and some of you resisted the call of God. God may have called you as a young person, or impressed you that He had a place for you on the mission field years ago. But you were diverted in the pursuit of your own plans. Maybe you sought to bargain with God and reasoned that you could serve Him here in America and have been faithful in that commitment. But meanwhile an unreached people group has remained unreached, and lost multitudes in a foreign land have died without even an opportunity to hear and respond to the gospel.

Resistance to God's call reflects indifference toward a lost world. It is disobedience to a sovereign God who has every right and claim on our lives. It indicates a self-centeredness that is more concerned for our own comfort and welfare than for the people of China, India, Malawi, or Brazil. And it is an expression of prejudice toward those of other races and cultures. Jonah did not want the people of Nineveh to repent. It wasn't that he was scared or equivocal about God's will. He hated the Ninevites and wanted God to rain down fire and judgment on them. In fact, he admits this is why he fled to Tarshish. When God relented in response to their repentance, we are told, "Jonah was greatly displeased and became furious. He prayed to the LORD: 'Please, LORD, isn't this what I said while I was still in my own country? That's why I fled toward Tarshish in the first place. I knew that You are a merciful and compassionate God, slow to become angry, rich in faithful love, and One who relents from [sending] disaster'" (Jon. 4:1–2). Is that not despicable? He admits the reason he fled is he knew if he went to Nineveh and proclaimed the word of the Lord these despised pagans would probably repent and God would have compassion on them.

We would probably never admit to that kind of extreme prejudice, but how many people are unwilling to consider missionary service because they are more concerned for their own comfort and prosperity? How many put a geographic restriction on where they are willing to go and how they are willing to serve God? God is bringing the world into our country, but how many churches flee to suburban Tarshish to minister to their own kind and abandon the mission field in cities and neighborhoods being populated by Hispanics, Middle Easterners, and Asians that need to know our Lord. I recently heard a speaker at a mission conference say, "How much do you have to hate someone to believe everlasting life is possible and not tell them?" You probably react and say, "I don't hate people of other nations and cultures." But it is certainly not love that compels us to hold on to our ethnocentric provincialism and neglect the lost cities of the world.

You may not have fled to Tarshish and been swallowed by a whale. But have you fled to success and been swallowed up by ambition? Have you fled to material comfort and been swallowed up by worldly values? Have you fled to a narrow worldview and been swallowed up by a geographic restriction on God's will?

Foolishly, Jonah thought he could flee from God's presence. You don't have to change your address to be disobedient; disobedience is to flee from God's presence for His face no longer shines on you. The blessed intimacy of fellowship with Him is severed when we respond to His call with anything other than, "Here am I; send me."

A Compassion Rewarded

We have seen a concern revealed and a call resisted, but the culmination of the story is a compassion rewarded. God did not give up. He pursued Jonah; and, just as He has with some of you, He gave Him a second chance. He repeated the call until Jonah, coughed up by the whale, reluctantly obeyed, went to Nineveh, and proclaimed the word of the Lord. And, in spite of his displeasure, God's compassion was rewarded in the city being spared.

Because of your obedience to go to some of the lost and wicked cities of the world, to go to the unreached people groups that are dying in sin and depravity, you can go with assurance that He goes with you. The power of the message will draw people to the Savior because you go with a message of repentance and salvation. As Paul declared in Colossians 1:6, "The gospel . . . is bearing fruit and growing all over the world." And God has chosen to give you the privilege of taking that good news to the Ninevehs of the world. Go in obedience, faithful to His calling, persistent in your witness, and with joy and confidence that you will see God's compassion rewarded in the nations and peoples of the world knowing our Lord Jesus Christ.

34

Compassion for the Multitudes

Matthew 9:35–38

Each of you being appointed tonight is aware of the challenging financial situation accompanying your appointment and the tenuous support available for sending additional missionaries. Others are deeply convinced of God's call to the mission field but are being deferred due to lack of resources. You should recognize the providence of God in being a part of a select group who have the privilege of proceeding to the field in obedience to God's call. With more limited numbers, it has become more imperative that those serving overseas be deployed to the most strategic personnel needs in our task of reaching a lost world for Jesus Christ.

It is also important that you go with resolve to be as effective as possible in the goal of evangelizing the lost, discipling believers, training leaders, and planting churches. Some will contribute to the task by filling support roles essential to a global strategy. Some of you will apply specialized skills and experiences to gain access to restricted people groups or to communicate God's love as teachers or through humanitarian ministries. Many of you will have the privilege of reaching someone who is hearing of Jesus for the first time, while others will be joining colleagues and national partners to facilitate a growing harvest in open witness.

You go as an incarnational witness. Your effectiveness will not be contingent on your abilities, gifts, and training, as important as that may be. Your success will be determined by the degree to which you reflect the presence of Jesus, allow your life to be a channel of the Holy Spirit's power, and emulate the model our Lord Himself established as He came to reveal God's love and establish His kingdom. The life you live and the love people see in you are what will open hearts and earn credibility for your verbal witness. A couple of verses in the Gospel of Matthew reveal the foundation for everything else you might do.

"Then Jesus went to all the towns and villages, teaching in their synagogues, preaching the good news of the kingdom, and healing every disease and every sickness. When He saw the crowds, He felt compassion for them, because they were weary and worn out, like sheep without a shepherd" (Matt. 9:35–36). This passage reflects four things to which you need to give attention—where you go, what you see, what you feel, and what you do.

Where You Go

Jesus went about all the cities and villages. When the Scripture says "all," it means *all*. It was important for everyone to have an opportunity to hear and respond to the gospel of the kingdom. There is significant controversy regarding the priority of our mission task. Some say we ought to concentrate our efforts where people are responsive—to populate heaven with as many souls as possible that can be saved. But to go only to the harvest fields—where missionaries can witness openly and be assured of response—would neglect most of the world and relegate multitudes to hell without an opportunity to hear and believe.

Not everyone responded to follow Jesus, but He was diligent to go to all the cities and villages, just as we must be faithful to engage all peoples with the message of salvation. As you go to your place of assignment, God will open doors of opportunity; you will establish relationships and likely begin to nurture one or more groups toward becoming followers of Jesus. Be faithful in that task, but don't ignore the multiethnic communities and places that are being neglected. Though your ministry will take diverse forms, don't neglect getting to the main thing—the message that Jesus came and died and rose again to save sinners, to forgive sin, to give a new life and eternal salvation.

What You See

Like Jesus, you will see the multitudes—more than you ever imagined could be gathered into a geographic entity. It is hard to imagine the massive population and congested crowds you will encounter. I grew up in a town of fifteen hundred people in Mississippi. It wasn't far from the capital city of Jackson, so I knew what a city was in terms of shopping centers, skyscrapers, and expressways in that metropolis of 200,000 people. In my Southern rural provincialism, I was ill prepared for encountering the seven million people of Jakarta upon my arrival in Indonesia, and the teeming multitudes, cacophony of sounds, and chaotic traffic congestion of Manila, Bangkok, Calcutta, and Mumbai. And these cities didn't begin to compare with places like Shanghai, Tokyo, Mexico City, and Sao Paulo, with populations approaching twenty million people. If the United States had the same population density of India, we would have three billion people. The little country of Bangladesh in South Asia is about the size of Arkansas, but has 140 million people! Some of you are going to China where you are likely to be in one of a 180 cities with more than a million people.

As you see the multitudes, it is easy to depersonalize the masses and go into a survival mode in which you isolate yourself and your family, venturing out into the market to purchase essential supplies and quickly retreating to the security of your apartment. You will find yourself becoming paranoid and suspicious of every stranger. Struggling to learn a new language, you will feel foolish and embarrassed each time your attempt to communicate is met with smirks and amusement. But I challenge you to take your eyes off yourself, your needs, and your problems and see the multitudes through the eyes of Jesus!

Yes, there are a lot of people, and they will be an irritant and inconvenience, but each one has a soul that desperately needs to be redeemed. Each one is an individual that is entrapped in bondage to sin and a worldview that has inhibited their ability to know God's love and the salvation He has provided. They are hurting from oppression, suffering every form of disease and affliction, often without access to medical treatment. You will find yourself in the midst of multitudes distressed, in despair and hopelessness, not only because of poverty, political oppression, and an unsanitary environment but because they are alienated from God.

WHAT YOU FEEL

Be prepared for the emotions you will experience when you encounter the multitudes. A natural reaction is fear, as you may feel insecure and threatened. You may feel anger at the inconvenience created in navigating the congested traffic, the beggars that constantly hound you in public places, and the inevitable noise and smells that are inescapable. Jesus responded with compassion, and it is expected you should as well.

That is easy to say, but it is unnatural to love the unlovely, to care for the repulsive, and to give oneself to the needs of others. We are basically self-centered creatures who tend to focus on our own needs, comforts, and security. Oh yes, we know what we ought to do as our Lord told us clearly to minister to the sick and lonely, visit the prisoner, feed the hungry. The Scripture says that pure and undefiled religion is to care for widows and orphans. More out of guilt and a sense of obligation, we occasionally reach out to the destitute and engage in a project among the homeless and those in need. After all, we are there to bear witness to the gospel, declare a message of hope and the good news of the kingdom. You will quickly rationalize that there is no way you can begin to meet all the needs around you so the tendency is not to meet any of them.

When Jesus saw the multitudes, He was moved with compassion for them. If you are not careful, you will find yourself feeling sorry for them but allowing your heart to grow calloused and indifferent. For you see, love is others-centered; it is not about us and our needs. Love motivates you to give of yourselves for the welfare of the beloved. That is not our nature, but God is love; it is His nature, and He has called us to become a channel of His love. As you go to the massive cities of Asia, Europe, and Latin America, the destitute villages of Africa and the unreached peoples of the world, the indwelling presence of Jesus goes with you. How would He see the people through you? He would see each one as created by God and an object of His love. He would see each one as someone for whom He died and shed His blood that they might no longer be distressed like sheep without a shepherd but would discover Him as the Good Shepherd who laid down His life for them.

What You Do

What do you do? You do what Jesus did among people distressed without purpose and hope in life, wandering in emptiness like sheep without a shepherd. You teach them the Word of God and proclaim the gospel of the kingdom. That's not just getting them to the point of praying a sinner's prayer and, having saved their souls, ignoring the needs of their lives. You identify with their suffering, bear their burdens, and minister healing to hearts that are hurting. You lead them to embrace a kingdom lifestyle in which they walk by faith and appropriate God's grace. You proclaim through word and deed the transformed life that only Jesus can give.

In a rural area of West Africa, one of our missionaries was working with a group of lay evangelists, challenging them to take the gospel to as many villages as possible. As he would return to the area and meet with them for training and encouragement each month, one of them would enthusiastically report on several more places believers had been baptized and churches started. When asked about the explanation for the response he was finding, this African simply replied, "The people are just waiting for good news!" Multitudes throughout the world are living in poverty, oppression, and even the more affluent without purpose and meaning in life. When they hear the good news of the kingdom, it is good news indeed.

Never forget that is how you are to respond. Regardless of your job assignment, you are to respond to the multitudes with compassion and never cease proclaiming the good news of the kingdom. In conclusion Jesus said, "The harvest is abundant, but the workers are few. Therefore, pray to the Lord of the harvest to send out workers into His harvest" (Matt. 9:37–38).

You will make a difference because of where you go, what you see, what you feel, and what you do. People are hungry to hear what the gospel provides. The world is filled with people in hopelessness and despair. They are following their religious traditions and cultural worldviews without any hope of relief from sin or assurance of eternal life. Where the gospel is being proclaimed, it is finding a responsive harvest, but how can people hear the good news unless there are workers to proclaim it and reap the harvest?

Those of you being appointed to missionary service are the result of God's call because someone pleaded in prayer for workers to be called to engage the nations, penetrate the lostness, and work the fields of the world. You have been obedient, but many more are needed if the harvest is to spread to every people and nation.

35

Commended as Servants of God

2 Corinthians 6:1–7

God is calling missionaries to overseas service today in a unique era of missions advance. Those being appointed are a part of a new generation that has the privilege of joining God as He works in unprecedented ways to fulfill His mission of being exalted among the nations. Following World War II, there was a phenomenal growth as new fields were opened and the harvest accelerated in a devastated and suffering world. Now, as we look back on the first decade of a new millennium, it is apparent God is using global events to extend His kingdom as never before. Creative access strategies have enabled us to engage unreached people groups and penetrate frontiers of lostness for the first time. In spite of strained international relationships and increasing religious opposition and hostility to our Christian witness, missionaries are being dispersed throughout the world to proclaim the solution for a world in spiritual darkness and despair.

There are those who look with admiration but also with sympathy on you for what you are doing. They see gifted, talented, successful ministers and professional people who have such potential for leading our churches and serving God in the comforts of our own society. It is a shame that you would leave all of that to serve in a remote corner of the world where you will likely encounter danger and hardship, isolated from family and loved ones. Some of your families just cannot understand why you would choose to take their grandchildren to the other side of the world and deprive grandparents, aunts, and uncles of the joy of sharing in life events. Some think you are being coerced into your assignment—I get letters frequently asking why we would make you serve in such a difficult location, as if God's will and your personal conviction of His leadership had nothing to do with the assignment.

In challenging you for the task you face, I want to highlight the exciting opportunity you will encounter and balance that with what it will require on your part. Our world today is not unlike the world in which the apostle Paul found himself as he sought to be obedient to God's calling. When Jesus sent out His followers to make disciples of all nations, it was in the fullness of time. From the foundation of the world, our sovereign God had been preparing and looking forward to this moment when redemption would be provided and the message of salvation would go out to all the world. A readiness for this good news and reception to the message swept Jerusalem, Judea, and Samaria and began to spread even among the Gentiles to the ends of the earth.

Yet, not unlike the world you will encounter, it was a world hostile to the message. Political powers and religious leaders conspired to squelch its spread, much like the government restrictions and religious opposition you will face. Those who dared to be obedient as witnesses were threatened, arrested, beaten, and even martyred. The irony was expressed by Paul in one of his letters, when he said, "Because a wide door for effective ministry has opened for me—yet many oppose me" (1 Cor. 16:9). Harvest and opposition go together.

This is reflected in the passage on which I want to focus your attention—2 Corinthians 6:1–7:

> Working together with Him, we also appeal to you:
> "Don't receive God's grace in vain." For He says: In an
> acceptable time, I heard you, and in the day of salvation,
> I helped you. Look, now is the acceptable time; look,
> now is the day of salvation. We give no opportunity
> for stumbling to anyone, so that the ministry will not
> be blamed. But in everything, as God's ministers, we
> commend ourselves: by great endurance, by afflictions,
> by hardship, by pressures, by beatings, . . . by patience,
> by kindness, by the Holy Spirit, by sincere love, by the
> message of truth, by the power of God.

RECOGNIZE YOU ARE A RECIPIENT OF GOD'S GRACE

Each one of you recognize that you were called by God's grace, and that grace was not in vain as you accepted it as the only means of your salvation. Others, even here in America, are still striving through their own efforts to know God, trying to live a good enough life to merit being received into heaven. They need to realize, as each of you, that no one is worthy or sufficient in their own works of righteousness to offset the sin nature that separates us from God. Only by the unmerited favor and grace of God can we be saved by acknowledging our sin and helplessness and coming to Him in repentance and faith. And you have found that God's grace is not in vain; it really did save and transform your life.

Having read your bio-data, I am aware that some of you really are trophies of grace. It is not only amazing that He would save you out of a rebellious, self-centered lifestyle, but His grace has called you to serve Him on the mission field; it is not necessarily because of your stellar character and resume. Others wanted to be here being appointed, but financial restraints have forced the limitation of the number of new missionaries who can be supported. It is a reflection of God's grace that you would be among those sent out at this time. Just as God's grace has not been in vain, it is what will sustain you and enable you to persevere and serve Him faithfully in the future.

If you are confident that you have what it takes and feel adequate in your own abilities, that will quickly change as you struggle to learn a new language and identify with a strange culture. But God's grace will enable you and your family to make the adjustments and will allow you to be used in spite of mistakes, conflicts, and discouragements. This is because, as Paul reflected, we work together with Christ. Because of His presence, His power, and His provision, you will be able to accomplish the task He has set before you.

GOD'S GRACE MAKES THIS A DAY OF SALVATION

Because of God's grace, we can testify with Paul in saying, "Now is the acceptable time; look, now is the day of salvation" (2 Cor. 6:2). I have often said that the last decade of the twentieth century saw a greater advance in global evangelization than the last two hundred years of modern missions. With the breakup of the Soviet Union and discovery of creative access strategies, there has been a new dimension of global harvest. But that pales in comparison to what we have seen God do since we entered the twenty-first century. Baptisms in our annual report have more than doubled and now exceed over half a million each year. Church growth rates have gone from 2 to 4 percent to double-digit growth, several years exceeding 20 percent. Last year twenty-four thousand new churches were started, and more than a hundred unreached people groups have been engaged with the gospel each year. People are not finding hope and assurance in their traditional religions and worldviews; they are looking for something that will give them security in the midst of warfare, chaos, and political upheaval. Indeed, now is the day of salvation! This is the acceptable time in God's providence to join Him in His mission to extend His salvation to all peoples.

The diversity of your assignments reflects that divine strategy. We cannot identify where most of you are going to serve, because you have been called to penetrate a door that is opening to unreached people groups, the neglected harvest where people have never before had access to the gospel. "This is the acceptable time!" Others of you have been called to nurture historic work on traditional open fields, strengthening Baptist partners and serving the institutions that are essential to growth and spreading the message of salvation. Yes, now is the day of salvation, and God's grace in providing redemption for a lost world will not be in vain because you go to extend His salvation to the ends of the earth.

DON'T DISCREDIT YOUR WITNESS AND MINISTRY

Because it is a time for harvest and such a unique opportunity for God's salvation to be proclaimed, it is important that you give no cause for offense and discredit the ministry and work of God lest His grace be in vain. You may be saying, "I wouldn't think of doing anything to discredit the work of God." But it is so easy to succumb to discouragement, conflict, and bitterness. It is easy to become self-centered and focus on your own needs and sense of entitlement, rather than having an attitude of sacrifice and dying to self. In the midst of congested crowds, tropical heat, bureaucratic red tape, and people who abuse and take advantage of you, it is easy to become impatient, unloving, and diverted from the reason you are there in the first place—to proclaim His salvation.

It isn't easy to persevere, to maintain a servant heart and bear the trials in the midst of discouragement, lack of appreciation, and lack of response. You will sometimes have to relinquish your own opinions and swallow your pride for the sake of cooperation and unity that mission strategies might go forward and the ministry not be discredited. You must recognize that there is a higher purpose, a more noble calling; it is the glory of God and salvation of the lost. It is not just a matter of fulfilling your job assignment but living in a way that your life is an incarnational witness of a living Savior. Ezekiel 36:23 says, "The nations will know that I am . . . the Lord GOD—'when I demonstrate My holiness through you in their sight.'" Our most powerful witness is when a lost world sees the holiness of God in our lives. Don't do anything that will cause offense to the gospel and discredit your ministry. Note how Paul says this will be done.

IN EVERYTHING COMMEND YOURSELVES AS SERVANTS OF GOD

You are God's witness where you go. Some of you will be the first Christian people that your city or community have ever seen. What are they going to observe, and what impression will it make as you live among them? Realize it is not about your success and what you are able to do; success in planting the gospel is contingent on the degree to which you are a servant of God. Only as you focus on others can God's purpose be fulfilled.

But notice how Paul indicates you are commended as servants. We can easily understand that it is in purity, patience, kindness, the Holy Spirit, genuine love, the word of truth, and the power of God; but that is not the total picture. Someone has said you can know if you truly have a servant heart by your attitude when people treat you like a servant! We could elaborate on the importance of reflecting each of these characteristics. It is obvious that you need to live a pure and holy life, avoiding temptations and compromise that might lead to moral failure. Genuine love is others centered instead of living for self; exhibiting kindness and patience toward others must characterize your life and ministry. It is essential you hold to the word of truth and sound doctrine if your witness is going to reflect the power of God.

But He also says you have been commended as servants in endurance, afflictions, hardships, distresses, tumults, labors, sleeplessness, and hunger. He actually goes on to list twenty-eight ways that commend your servanthood. It's a strange list. You will have times of distress; Jesus said, "You will have suffering in this world" (John 16:33). How will you handle it—in a natural carnal response, or as a servant of Christ? You will go through the tumult of conflicts, with others and within your own soul, issues that are so emotionally burdensome that you toss and turn through sleepless nights. It goes with the territory of being a servant of Christ called to proclaim His salvation.

In each emeritus recognition service of retiring missionaries, there are those who have lost a child or spouse, or been through a debilitating illness, but they endured, faithful to the end. Currently we are dealing with situations where visas are being denied, and missionaries are living with uncertainty. You will face hardships in living through political disruption and social upheaval. Having a servant heart and recognizing you are nothing but a bond slave of Jesus Christ is what will enable you not to give offense to the gospel. Don't let God's grace, that is being poured out in abundance to you, be in vain. This is the acceptable time when God is moving; this is the day of salvation for a lost world. You are blessed to have the privilege of commending yourselves as His servants as you declare His salvation to the ends of the earth.

36

Aligned with God's Mission

Romans 15:18–21

With mixed emotions I come to the last missionary appointment service as president of the International Mission Board. There have been one hundred services such as this over the last seventeen years of my tenure. Along with short-term categories of missionary service, more than ten thousand new personnel have been sent to take the gospel all over the world. I have been able to observe the factors that result in effectiveness in the mission task. Most important, collectively and individually, are vision, focus, and passion.

There must be a vision that proclaiming the gospel of Christ will, indeed, draw a lost world to our Savior. There must be a vision that sees the kingdoms of this world becoming the kingdom of our Lord. Effectiveness demands that we remain focused on the main purpose of our mission and calling. It is easy to get diverted and for one's time to be consumed in doing many things that are good but don't move us toward the objective of redemption and all peoples worshipping and exalting God. In all the adjustments you face on the mission field, you can get diverted and consumed with survival and all that living in a foreign country entails.

You must be focused on a mission that is consistent with God's purpose, characterized by God's power, and compelled by God's passion. This is reflected in the apostle Paul's testimony in Romans 15:18–21: "For I would not dare say anything except what Christ has accomplished through me to make the Gentiles obedient by word and deed, by the power of miraculous signs and wonders, and by the power of God's Spirit. As a result, I have fully proclaimed the good news about the Messiah from Jerusalem all the way around to Illyricum. So my aim is to evangelize where Christ has not been named, in order that I will not be building on someone else's foundation, but, as it is written: Those who had no report of Him will see, and those who have not heard will understand."

Your Mission Must Be Consistent with God's Purpose

Paul expressed the vision and compelling passion of his life and mission as being consistent with God's purpose for all peoples to hear and understand the gospel. That's why he aspired to preach the gospel, not where Christ was already known, but where those who had not heard the good news would have an opportunity to hear and understand. We get a lot of criticism regarding our emphasis on engaging unreached people groups and deploying missionaries to places not yet receptive to the gospel. Researchers tell us there are still more than a billion people who have yet to hear of Jesus. They are isolated culturally and geographically in places where there are no churches and no Christian believers to be a witness. There is no Scripture in their language, and no missionary has engaged them with the gospel.

Many think we ought to focus on reaping a harvest and concentrate personnel in places where people are responsive. Certainly God desires as many as possible to be saved, but if we concentrated our witness where people already had access to the gospel, most of the world would be neglected and never have an opportunity to be saved. That would hardly fulfill the mandate to "preach the good news to everyone" (Mark 16:15), "be [His] witnesses . . . to the ends of the earth" (Acts 1:8), or to "make disciples of all nations" (Matt. 28:19). Others continue to emphasize the priority of reaching the lost where we live; and, in fact, that is why most of the resources of our churches are concentrated on America and our own communities where there are already many churches and everyone has access to the gospel.

On my last trip to Central Asia, I was thrilled to see that the gospel had been planted among twenty-three of the major people groups in this region—people who for centuries had been in bondage to their Islamic faith and then prohibited religious freedom as a part of the former Soviet Union. When I asked how many people groups had yet to be engaged with a Christian witness, I was told there are more than three hundred ethnic-language groups that had not yet even heard the name of Jesus. That is hard for us to comprehend in this age of technology and communication when we can see news events as they occur simultaneously all over the world. The regional leader told me, with tears in his eyes, that the most difficult thing about being responsible for our mission work in that part of the world was limited personnel and resources. Every year in their annual strategic planning, they had to decide which of those people groups would be deprived of hearing the gospel yet another year, realizing many would die before they ever heard the news that a Savior had died for them. I came home from that trip with the question burning in my heart, "By what criteria should any people group be deprived of at least hearing the gospel when God has blessed us so richly in numbers, resources, and the potential in our lives of reaching the whole world?"

Some of you are going to join colleagues already at work in strategies to plant the gospel where missionaries have been laboring. But many of you are being assigned to unreached people groups and have the privilege of being the one to impact them with the gospel for the first time. Whatever the situation, never forget your mission personally must be consistent with God's purpose that all people hear and understand the gospel. God is not willing for any to perish. That's why He called Abraham to leave his home and family, so that through his seed "all the nations of the earth will be blessed" (Gen. 18:18). He called Israel as His chosen people to "proclaim His salvation from day to day. Declare His glory among the nations" (1 Chron. 16:23–24). And that is why Jesus has called us and sent us to the nations. It is not about your assignment and job description; it is about planting your life among people who are lost. Keep pushing to the edge, evangelizing to the fringes, penetrating the remaining pockets of lostness until all have had an opportunity to hear, understand, and respond to the gospel.

Your Mission Must Be Characterized by God's Power

Paul had been faithful in the task; in fact, he observed that he had proclaimed the gospel among the Gentiles from Jerusalem to Illyricum. That was all across the provinces of Asia and European civilization to northern Italy. That did not mean everyone had been saved, but many had received the message, believers were being discipled, and the churches that had resulted were continuing to spread the witness. Paul testified that even though he was the instrument God chose to use, it was not him and what he did but the work of the Holy Spirit that had brought about such an extensive harvest. He had seen God validate the truth of the gospel through signs and wonders.

We have reported how God is moving throughout the world in unprecedented ways. Previously closed and restricted people groups are being engaged with the gospel for the first time and are responding. We used to think they were unreached because they were resistant to the gospel, but to the contrary, they had just never heard! New believers being baptized on mission fields overseas have doubled in the last ten years, and church-planting movements are multiplying. This is not happening because of the genius of our mission strategy or because Western diplomacy has created a favorable environment for spreading the gospel. To the contrary, the world is increasingly hostile to a Christian witness. Religious worldviews and government restrictions continue to create barriers. But God is using global events—warfare, political disruption, economic uncertainty, and natural disasters—to turn the hearts of the people to a search for hope and security and spiritual answers that only Jesus can provide. It is an awesome experience to be in a position to have a global overview of what God is doing throughout the world; those involved with the IMB know we are not making it happen. We are scrambling for all we are worth to keep up with what God is doing in the world today in the power of His Spirit.

Wherever Jesus is lifted up in a bold, positive witness, people will be drawn to salvation. Several years ago, a missionary shared the gospel with a Muslim young man in a South Asian village. He eventually became a believer and began to share his faith and convictions with others. Today that movement claims half a million Muslim-background believers following Christ. Just last week, I read of churches multiplying in Mongolia as a result of the faithful witness of a short-term doctor who went to serve the medical needs of this deprived country but was also faithful to share Jesus with colleagues and friends. One of our personnel reported a baptismal service in which more than a hundred new converts identified with Jesus where previously the young man had been the only Christian.

You can be assured that you don't go out to serve in your own strength. While training and education are important, that is not what will convince people of the truth of the gospel and transform lives. Before Jesus sent His followers to disciple the nations, He assured them that all power had been given to Him in heaven and earth. And He promised to go with them with all the power and authority the Father had bestowed upon Him. We have hope of effectively being His witnesses to the ends of the earth because we have received the power of the Holy Spirit within us. Your mission must not be simply a reflection of creative strategies, faithful labor to implement good works and ministries, or efforts based on your appealing personality and persuasive communication. It must be characterized by God's power.

YOUR MISSION MUST BE COMPELLED BY GOD'S PASSION

Right now you are highly motivated to go to the mission field in obedience to God's call to impact a lost world for Jesus Christ. It has been determined that you are qualified for cross-cultural witness and ministry. Though you still face a few weeks of orientation and further preparation, you are ready to do whatever it takes to reach your city, people group, nation, and affinity peoples. Your motivation may be based on a conscientiousness of being obedient to God's will. Most of you have already served in short-term assignments or been on mission trips, and your life was impacted by the overwhelming lostness you encountered. You saw the poverty and spiritual darkness, the hopelessness of people without Christ, and are compelled by the need to do something about it.

But what compels you in the task—that which enables you to persevere—has to go beyond a response to the need or a sense of obligation to what God has called you to do. You must be compelled by the passion that God has for His glory among the nations. It was a passion that compelled Him to give His Son to die on the cross and pay the penalty of sin for a lost world. This was the passion that drove Paul, and the other disciples before him, to take the gospel to the nations in spite of threats, imprisonment, being beaten and stoned and even martyred. He explained this to the church at Corinth when he wrote, "Christ's love compels us" (2 Cor. 5:14). It caused every other activity, pursuit, and personal concern to fade to insignificance as he testified, "I determined to know nothing among you except Jesus Christ and Him crucified" (1 Cor. 2:2). Paul summed up this passion in his farewell address to the elders in Ephesus: "But I count my life of no value to myself, so that I may finish my course and the ministry I received from the Lord Jesus, to testify to the gospel of God's grace" (Acts 20:24). This was the life verse of Lottie Moon, one which compelled her to give of her life that the people of China might be assimilated into the kingdom of God.

That kind of passion will enable you to endure the hardships and adversity you will inevitably face. God's passion for a lost world planted in your heart will keep you focused and willing to pay the cost of difficult adjustments and language learning. That is what enables you to say good-bye to family and friends and leave the comfortable lifestyle in America to embrace the isolation and deprivation that will come in Third-World countries. When Americans are threatened with kidnapping or become victims of terrorist violence, we often have to explain why missionaries would go to dangerous places; it is the only way people can know Jesus and the hope He provides. You don't go out of a sense of adventure or because someone has got to do it but because you are compelled by God's passion for a lost world.

You have been called of God and have responded in obedience. You are being commissioned tonight to go to the ends of the earth, supported by the prayers and the gifts of Southern Baptists. As you go, be sure your mission is consistent with God's purpose, is characterized by God's power, and is compelled by God's passion.

MORE BOOKS BY JERRY RANKIN

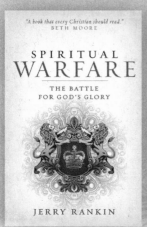

Spiritual Warfare
A Battle for God's Glory

Rankin, as witness to spiritual warfare around the world, helps readers understand the feelings of resentment, anfer, doubt, pride, and adversity as darts of deception thrown by Satan. The book becomes an inspiring guide to the Spirit-filled life, illuminating spritual disciplines that equip us for victory.

Paperback // 304 pages
ISBN: 978-0-8054-4880-1
Retail Price: $19.99

In the Secret Place
A Pilgriamge Through the Psalms

In the Secret Place gathers devotions and prayers written by Rankin for each of the one hundred fifty chapters in the book of Psalms. Personal yet universsal, they reflect an openhearted journey of faith and deepening love for God to which the reader will aspire.

Paperback // 352 pages
ISBN: 978-0-8054-4881-8
Retail Price: $14.99

Spiritual Warfare and Missions
A Battle for God's Glory
Among the Nations

Jerry Rankin and Ed Stetzer

Rankin, with noted missiologist Ed Stetzer, calls out Satan's ongoing strategy to convince Christians that the Great Commission is optional. But for every evil sucess, Rankin and Stetzer point to where Satan is failing, encouraging readers to renew their passion to declare God's glory among the nations.

Paperback // 328 pages
ISBN: 978-0-8054-4887-0
Retail Price: $19.99